Thy Kingdom Come

Life in the Millennial Age

Tom Grantham
5/30/2017

How marvelous is the plan of God for His Children!

Tom Grantham

I Cor 2:9

"Thy Kingdom Come"

All Scripture quotations are taken from the Authorized King James Version of the Scriptures.

"Thy Kingdom Come" is a work of fiction. Similarities between the characters or situations depicted in this book and any real person living or dead is purely coincidental.

Published by TNG Publishing
1508 Preston Street, Opelika, AL 36801

Published in the United States of America

Cover photography by Seth McKelvey

ISBN: 13: 978-1545342169
ISBN: 10: 1545342164

Fiction/Religious/Prophecy

DEDICATION

This book is dedicated to two groups of people.

The Pastors and teachers who challenged me over the years and instilled in my heart a love for the Scriptures and a desire to know the plan of God for the future.

Christians who love God and have committed your lives to Him, but have not given much thought to the plans He has made for your future. It is my humble desire that at some point in the reading of this book, your own imaginations will be set on fire by the Holy Spirit and you will have a new appreciation and anticipation for what is in store for us.

FOREWORD

As you read this book – as I certainly hope you will! – there are some things of which you need to be aware.

This book was not written to be used as a communication of theological doctrine. While I have made every attempt to avoid any speculation that would be contrary to Scripture, I have used quite a bit of artistic license in interpreting and projecting how the descriptions of life in the Millennial Kingdom might be played out. (I have included an appendix at the end of the book where I discuss my different interpretations and give the Scripture references that guided my thinking.)

So, if my purpose is not the communication of doctrine, what is the purpose of this book?

Over the last few years, I have come to realize that the majority of the Church, even those in fundamental, Bible-preaching ones, seems woefully ignorant of God's plan for our future. Their understanding of the plan of God for His people seems to be, "We live, we die, then we go to Heaven." There is little or no comprehension of the life that awaits us in the Kingdom Age, even though there is much, much more information that is revealed in Scripture concerning this age than there is concerning our eternal existence.

Even much of our concept of "Heaven" is derived from John's description of the New Jerusalem. Our thoughts, particularly as reflected in our songs and much of our teaching about Heaven, focus on the streets of gold, the walls of jasper, the gates of pearl, the river of life. All of these come directly from John's description of the city of God.[1] And this city does not make its appearance until after the Kingdom Age! In other words, if your idea of Heaven is the experiencing of the sights and wonders of the New Jerusalem, you're at least 1,007 years away from Heaven – seven years for the period known as the Tribulation, and one thousand years for the reign of Christ on earth!

I feel like this has left many with a distorted perspective on the life we now live. If we cannot visualize the concept of the Millennial Kingdom, we are likely to feel that there are experiences here on earth that we will miss if we do not grasp them during our brief stay here. There are so many places to visit, so many natural wonders to see that no one will ever be able to experience them all in one brief lifetime. However, when we realize that we have a thousand years, unencumbered by the restrictions of finance or schedule, unburdened by the demands of work and responsibilities, a whole new horizon of opportunities presents itself. This book is written to help you with that visualization.

In addition, there are those who feel cheated by the early death of a loved one. When we lose someone at an early age, there is a tendency to feel like we have lost opportunities. We did not have the time together we would have liked to develop the relationship and share one another's company. However, if you are saved, if you both are children of God, then you will have multiple lifetimes to enjoy and revel in each other's lives.

And finally, for those of you who are not confident that you are born again and are not assured that you are going to be present to enjoy the wonders of the Kingdom, it is my earnest prayer that the picture painted will be so grand that it will motivate you to "make your calling and election sure"[2], to have no doubt but that you are saved and prepared to meet the Lord. You certainly do not want to miss out on what is sure to be the adventure of a lifetime! (Remember that no matter how wonderful the life portrayed in these pages may be, God's plan is infinitely greater than anything we mortals might imagine!)

And so we begin our journey. It is my prayer that as we stroll through the Millennial Kingdom together, you will see yourself and your family, reunited and enjoying the bounty that has been provided by our Creator and Savior.

Welcome to your new home!

---

[2] II Peter 1:10

PROLOGUE

Ross Waters served as Pastor of Longview Baptist Church just outside of Raleigh, North Carolina for seventeen years, alongside his wife of thirty-eight years, his high school sweetheart, Jessica. He had faithfully preached the gospel, prayed, served...and watched as the congregation had dwindled, and his community had followed the lead of the nation in becoming more and more secular. They had truly reached the last days the Bible had prophesied about, when people would seek out preachers who would tickle their ears rather than preach the truth.[3]

They were driving home from a particularly discouraging Sunday service. The crowd had been smaller than usual, and an argument had actually broken out among some of the members concerning the songs that had been selected for the service.

"How much longer can it be?" Jessica asked. "Surely the Lord is coming soon. The whole world is so wicked. It's even invaded the church."

"I know," Ross agreed. "Since the last election things have spiraled downward so quickly. Things were already headed in the wrong direction in the U. S. and it just accelerated after the election."

---

[3] II Timothy 4:3

7

"We knew it would, but I never expected things to fall apart so quickly."

"Well, the economy had been teetering on the verge of collapse for so long, and when it finally crashed the whole world was thrown into chaos. The Russians saw an opportunity to expand their influence in the Middle East, and we were in no position to do anything about it. I'm not sure we would have anyway given the current political climate in Washington. Without a proper Biblical perspective on Israel, everything is viewed from the standpoint of what is best for the nation economically or politically."

She sighed. "I just never thought we would see the day that we would not come to the aid of Isra.."

It had happened in a flash. So quickly as to be indescribable. The Scripture had said it would be – "in a moment, in a twinkling of an eye."[4] It was a day just like any other – just a normal day. There was a sound like a loud clap of thunder. They could hear it reverberating through the atmosphere, echoing in the distance behind them – becoming fainter and fainter.

THE REMAINDER OF THE STORY IS FROM THE PERSPECTIVE OF ROSS WATERS

It took a few seconds for me to realize what was happening. The immediate sensation was similar to what I might have imagined if I were sucked up into the

---

[4] I Corinthians 15:52

middle of a tornado. I could sense that I was moving, flying, speeding through the air at incredible speed, yet not the least bit alarmed or afraid. What seemed like a few moments passed before I was able to focus.

Then I saw Him!

The first thing I noticed was the brightness. It was as if I were staring directly into the sun on a bright summer day, yet for some reason my eyes were able to focus. As I did, I could see that indeed it was Christ. I had obviously never seen Him before, yet there was no doubt as to His identity. The brightness was actually emanating from Him. Like pulsing waves of energy, the light flowed out from Him in ever-increasing circles until it engulfed me.

My soul cried out to Him. It was only then that I noticed the others. I had been so captivated by the appearance of Christ that I had not even noticed that I was one among millions who were soaring to meet Him. But as I heard my own voice praise Him, I became conscious that it was only one of a great chorus. I remembered on earth thinking that at this moment I would look around to see my family and loved ones caught up with me. But I could not take my eyes off of Him. My attention – indeed my very being – was drawn to Him as metal filings are drawn to a powerful magnet.

Suddenly I became aware that we all were now hurtling through space at unimaginable speed, seeing stars, and then galaxies flash by, as we went deeper and deeper into space. Bursting through the outer rim of the universe, I found myself in a place of utter tranquility.

There are no human words to describe it. I stood on what appeared to be a solid body of water. Waves of energy pulsated around me, reminding me of the heat waves sometimes seen rising up from the pavement on a hot summer day on earth. Only there was no heat. Not that it was cold. There was no sensation of temperature at all. I was at one with this environment.

All the others had vanished. I had no idea where they had gone, or for that matter, where I was. For the first time since this began, I became conscious of my own self. My "body" was very different from what I remembered. There was a physical nature to it, yet there was a new element to this being.[5] My senses were heightened. I remembered as we were speeding through space, that I had been able to see the different solar systems as they passed by, even though we must have been traveling at many times the speed of light.

Not only was there no sense of pain or discomfort, but I somehow knew that there would never be again. This body did not have the capacity to feel such things. Instead, there was a sense of power, and an overwhelming sensation of peace and confidence. Although I did not know where I was, or what was about to happen, I felt absolutely no apprehension.

_____

[5] I Corinthians 15:35-44

I have no idea how much time passed. Rather, I should say, it was that there was no time. I was just there – in that moment. And then, He was there! Although I could not see Him, I sensed His energy. The very air pulsated with His presence. A panorama opened before me, and as I looked, I recognized scenes from my life on earth. At once, I knew what was happening – where I was – why it was only me.

This was the Judgment Seat of Christ![6]

This was not at all what I imagined. In my earthbound thinking, I had envisioned a giant throne with everyone gathered before the Lord. One by one, we would be called before Him to give account of our lives on earth.

Instead, it was just me…and Him.

The scenes began to unfold. Things that I thought were long buried were recalled in vivid detail. Far too many were of times when I had failed. My spirit shuddered each time I saw myself speak in anger, or act in selfishness. I literally cringed as I watched occasions when I succumbed to temptation. Equally grievous were the missed opportunities. There were countless occasions where I had a chance to witness, either through the sharing of the gospel or just through a good deed done in the name of Christ. I watched as many of these passed without action.

---

[6] II Corinthians 5:10

And with each of these, I sensed a loss. It is difficult to describe. It was a regret coupled with a feeling of what might have been. What impact might I have had on others for the cause of Christ if only I had seized each and every opportunity? What joy had I forfeited the times that I had selfishly chosen my own way over Christ's? The sorrow was so intense it was akin to physical pressure. I recalled from the Scripture Paul's writing about this time – of works of wood, hay and stubble being consumed by fire. "*And if any man's work shall be burned, he shall suffer loss...*"[7]

There were only two things that kept the situation from being unbearable.

The first is difficult to put into words. Along with the regret came a sense of...relief? It was similar to the feeling I remembered from my earthly experience when I had done something wrong and only I knew about it. When I was finally able to share it, to ask forgiveness and to have it put behind me, it would bring with it a sense of relief. Each of those scenes from my past left me feeling sorrowful, yet in some sense washed, as though He had now seen me in all my weaknesses and failures, but was still there. Each instance was somehow a reminder that His love was unconditional, that He had always known that I was imperfect, and yet had still chosen me for His own.

---

[7] I Corinthians 3:15

The second thing was the other scenes. There were times – not as many as I would have liked, at this point – but times nonetheless, when I had indeed moved as directed by the Spirit. These were also reviewed. At each of these, when I had followed His leading, as the event would unfold before me, I could hear Him whisper in my spirit, 'Well done.'[8]

The first time I heard it, it was like a wave of euphoria sweeping over my being. Never had I imagined that a spoken word could thrill me so! With each occasion, the intensity would increase. I wanted this to go on and on. I wished that there had been hundreds and thousands more times when I had followed the Spirit's leading, for at this moment nothing else could possibly have mattered as much as hearing Him speak those words.

Several times along the way, I sensed something at my feet. When the process was completed, I looked down to see what appeared to be sparkling crowns. My first thought was one of embarrassment. I had failed so often and accomplished so little that it seemed inappropriate to be rewarded. How gracious is our Lord!

Then the process was done. I had no concept of the passage of time. Did this all occur in an instant? Or did it take a lifetime? Does either of those words have meaning still?

_____

[8] I Corinthians 3:14

Once more, I became aware of my own self. Something had changed. There was a feeling of purity. Every fault and blemish had been eradicated. I was at one with the Savior. His essence now saturated my being. His light permeated every cell. I was clean and whole and wonderfully alive!

Instantly I was in the presence of the other saints. We were all somehow aware that each of us had just experienced the same thing. We had each had our time before the Judge of all the earth, and now we were reunited. Christ once more appeared, His radiance more spectacular than ever.

As the shouts of praise and adoration began, the crowns that had been given were cast at His feet. Now that seemed appropriate! All that had been accomplished during our earthly pilgrimage had been the results of His grace and empowering. This was the greatest joy of any that had been experienced up to this time – to be able to take the rewards that had been given and return them to the One who had made it all possible.

"Worthy! Worthy is the Lamb! Worthy! Worthy is the Lamb!"

The shouts continued for what seemed like years. But then again, there was really no sensation of the passing of time at all. As the praise began to ebb, Jesus disappeared, leaving us to resume the renewing of acquaintances with one another.

How strange earthly thoughts seemed at this point. I had envisioned a mortal scenario, scouring the landscape, looking for family and friends with which to reunite. Rather, it was just a matter of thinking – and I knew instantly where each one was. By simply willing it to be so, we could be together. And so began the process of reconnecting.

Spouses, children, parents and grandparents, friends – one by one they were reunited, each reunion bringing its own measure of joy and exhilaration. Again, there was no sense of time. There was no hurry. There was no feeling of any deadline or need to cut any experience short. Each one was enjoyed individually and to its fullest.

The love shared on earth had been so limited. We all recognized it immediately. All earthly emotions had been corrupted by the fall and the curse of sin. Humans could never fully and freely love because of their own fallenness. Always in their minds was that taint of selfishness. We would love if we were loved. We would only invest so much of ourselves because to invest all was to risk tremendous pain. We did not want to be hurt or rejected.

Now all that was gone. There was no more fear. There were no more doubts. There were no feelings of insecurity or concern about how we were perceived by others. There was only pure, unbridled love. For the first time we experienced *agape*, God's highest and purest expression of Himself.

As we reveled in this new reality, we gradually came to an awareness of other activities. Because there was no sense of time, there is no way to describe how long it was before we came to this realization. In one sense, it seemed so long since we had been "earth bound" that it was almost as if we were never there. And yet in another sense, we were "just there."

It was then that we noticed him for the first time – a supernatural being who had been observing our activities. There was something about him that seemed to invite us into his presence, so we approached him.

"Greetings to you," he said. "Welcome to your new home."

(I am using earth language to describe things for which there are no other words. When I say, "he said", he actually did not "speak" as we would know it. He "communicated" thoughts, and they were received and understood. There was also no sense of a particular language. It wasn't as if he were speaking in Hebrew, or English, or Spanish, or Chinese or any other earthly language. He communicated ideas and thoughts – they were understood. I also refer to him as "he", although there was no real way of discerning whether this being were male or female. His essence was more one of pulsating energy than of flesh and bone or any other physical material.)

"You're an angel," I said.   It wasn't really a question – just a statement. I knew it to be true.

"That is correct. You may call me Aleph." (It was Hebrew for "teacher", but was also a derivative of a word that meant "thousand". We would later come to find out there was significance in each of those meanings.) "I am here to help you and your family get acclimated. Each group has their own guide."

I was thrilled to hear that. I had a number of questions, as I'm sure everyone else did.

Jessica spoke up first. "Where is God? The Father? We have seen Jesus a number of times. When will we see the Father? And what about the Holy Spirit?"

"If you have seen the Son, you have seen the Father.[9] He is the physical manifestation of all that is Yahweh.[10] You will come to learn more and more of the essence of God throughout eternity, for He is infinite. For now, understand that Yahweh is spirit.[11]   He reveals Himself through His Son. His Divine Essence surrounds you in the Person of the Holy Spirit. He is everywhere because it is His energy that comprises all that is in the universe.

"The followers of Hinduism were on the right track when they said that God is everything, and everything is

---

[9] John 14:9
[10] Colossians 1:15; 2:9
[11] John 4:24

God. However, they missed the key element of His physical manifestation of Himself in Yeshua, and the revelation of this truth in His word, the Bible. The Jehovah's Witnesses with their emphasis on kingdom teaching had a better grasp on the era you are about to enter than most Christians, yet they added human elements that diluted the message of grace and were wrong about the divine nature of Yeshua. You will find that virtually all of the religions of the world had some element of the truth in them. Deception is much easier if it comes wrapped in a veneer of truth."

"I see," she said, though we still found it somewhat difficult to grasp.

From the back of our group came, "How many are there like you?"

For the first time, Aleph seemed to show the earthly semblance of a smile. "There is none exactly like me. We were each created as unique entities. If you mean how many angels are there, there was originally one created for each star in the universe."

There was a short gasp from those gathered around. The latest estimate prior to our leaving earth was that there was more than a septillion stars. That's one, followed by 24 zeros! That was a number that was difficult for even our transformed minds to comprehend.

I was the next to speak up.

"I'm somewhat surprised at the appearance of my family and friends. I thought when we arrived here that our physical appearances would be changed more. I certainly did not expect my parents and grandparents to appear as old as they do. I thought they would look like they did when they were younger. I certainly didn't expect the eyeglasses and other signs of aging."

Aleph's answer was nothing less than astounding. "You will come to realize that physical appearance is in the eye of the beholder. You see them in that manner because that is the way you remember and relate to them. Others perceive them in different ways. You know as you are known.[12] You see your children and grandchildren as you remember them from earth.

"As you get more attuned to this heavenly realm, you will discover an amazing ability. You can change how you perceive others, and thus experience different types of relationships with them. You and your children may want to recapture relationships you had when they were young children, which you will be able to do when you both coordinate your perceptions of each other to that period of time. You are not bound by the physical. Your soul – the essence of who you are – remains the same regardless of what physical form you manifest yourself in, or how others perceive you."

---

[12] I Corinthians 13:12

This was an awesome realization. As I looked back at my family, it was true. I could literally change the way they appeared to me just by thinking. I could view them as they had been at any point in time on earth, just by willing it.

I remembered passages of Scripture relating to Jesus' appearance following the resurrection. When He first appeared to the disciples, it was in the form they had most recently seen Him, complete with the wounds of the cross – the nail-pierced hands and the wounded side that He had shown to Thomas.[13] Later on the Emmaus road, His identity was hidden from two of His followers until He chose to reveal it.[14] Then when He appeared to John on the Isle of Patmos, it was a different manifestation altogether – one revealing more of His majesty.[15] All of these were the same person with different physical appearances. Having been given a body like the Lord, I now had a similar ability.

Everyone was receiving the same information, and this spawned a new wave of interaction with each other as we leaped from time to time in our relationships with one another. At one moment Jessica and I could be holding our newborn son, and then immediately interact with our grown son and his own twin children.

Amazing!

---

[13] John 20:27
[14] Luke 24:16,31
[15] Revelation 1:12-16

I have no idea how long we spent engaging in this newfound ability. Time was obviously an "earth thing" and had no relevance to what we were experiencing.

At some point, our attentions were turned from our interactions with one another to a flurry of activity that was outside of our new environment. We had access to a heavenly view and perspective of what had been transpiring on earth since our departure. We all instinctively knew that those who had been left behind had been experiencing a time of great trial. The man of sin, the antichrist had taken over the kingdoms of the earth.[16] Our hearts grieved as we saw the result of his godless rule.

Unbridled by the restraint of the Holy Spirit, and without the preserving influence of the body of Christ, the world had become a cesspool of wickedness. Corruption and debauchery were rampant. Death and danger lurked around every corner, especially for those who resisted the will of the antichrist.

From our heavenly perspective, we were able to see how the years had progressed. From the time of the rapture, the world had been thrown into chaos. Economies had collapsed; anarchy and lawlessness had erupted; governments had been totally ineffective in controlling the populace. It appeared that the final chapter of humankind would be a tale of animal

---

[16] Revelation 13:1-8

savagery, killing and feeding on one another until they were all eradicated.

Then he had appeared.

Intelligent, charismatic, seemingly above the chaos and turmoil, he carried with him a confidence that had inspired the masses. Perhaps there was hope yet. He seemed to think so. And his hope hypnotized - possibly because there was so little hope to be found. The people flocked to him. The world leaders, desperate for some means to salvage their societies, were willing to do anything, to sacrifice anything for a chance at survival.

He had quickly assumed control of the United Nations and its forces, and almost overnight became the single most powerful government figure the world had ever known.[17] The world had no idea that they had installed Satan himself as their leader. We watched as the scroll of Bible prophecies was unrolled before us.

This man of sin had ratified a treaty with Israel signaling the beginning of Daniel's seventieth week, that seven-year period that would complete the 490 years of judgment against Israel that had been revealed to Daniel in chapter nine of his writings.[18] This ratification of the treaty alleviated the fear and destruction that had become rampant in the days following the rapture.

---

[17] Daniel 8:23-25; Revelation 13:1-8
[18] Daniel 9:24-27

The first three and a half years saw its share of problems – economic collapse, famines, rampant disease and death. And of course the relentless persecution of anyone who resisted the will of the antichrist – especially those who would name the name of Christ.

Nevertheless, there was hope among some that the world could endure. This hope was maintained and fueled by the constant bombardment by the media proclaiming the recovery and prosperity were just around the corner – as long as everyone followed the rules and regulations that issued forth from the throne room of earth's newest dictator.

Then came the abomination of desolation,[19] when the antichrist did the unspeakable. Marching into the reconstructed temple, he entered the inner sanctum, the Holy of Holies, the place where God manifested His presence to Israel. There he had proclaimed himself to be God. He was not only to be obeyed – he was to be worshiped!

Another leader had emerged, known in Scripture as the "false prophet."[20] He led a worldwide religion that acknowledged the Antichrist as divine. He directed all to worship him as such. The symbol of acknowledgement and acceptance of him was a mark received in your palm or forehead. Without this mark,

---

[19] Daniel 9:27; Matthew 24:15-21
[20] Revelation 13:11-18; 19:20

you were unable to engage in any type of commerce.[21] You were officially an enemy of the state.

That signaled the beginning of the final three and a half years of horrendous judgments on the inhabitants of the earth.[22] Wave after wave of unspeakable horrors were unleashed on the earth's population, reminiscent of the plagues that had been visited on Egypt as God had worked through Moses to rescue the Israelites from bondage.

As in the case of the plagues, they were intended as warnings and calls to repentance. Many saw them as such, and did indeed repent and turn to God. For the vast majority, however, they were only reasons to rebel and blaspheme even more.[23] Anger, resentment, despair and panic drove them to depths of vileness and violence that had never been experienced.

As we watched these final scenes unfold, we became aware of a rumbling in the heavens. Something was about to happen. The scene on earth was approaching a climax. The rulers of the eastern world, restless under the rule of the antichrist, had amassed a huge army and were approaching Jerusalem to engage the army of the antichrist.[24]

---

[21] Revelation 13:16-18
[22] Revelation 8,9
[23] Revelation 9:20-21; 16:9
[24] Daniel 11:44; Revelation 16:12

The mood in Heaven had changed. Suddenly we again saw the Lord. But now He looked different than before.[25] Astride a great white battle stallion, with fire in His eyes and an aura of majestic power about Him, He raised His hand and signaled for Gabriel to sound the trumpet call that would summon His saints. As wave after wave of glorified saints gathered, myriads of heavenly steeds appeared. Majestic in appearance, shimmering in the reflection of Christ's glory, they waited to be mounted by the saints. As far as the eye could see in every direction, millions upon millions of the saints of God, along with a countless number of the heavenly hosts of angels, had responded to the trumpet call. When all were ready, the sound of the trumpet once more pierced the atmosphere.

Then the heavens opened...

Christ Himself led the charge as we literally poured out of Heaven and descended toward the earth like a great tsunami. While our exit had appeared to take us through the constellations, our return was as if we were entering from another dimension. As we came through the rift between heaven and earth, we saw the battle scene unfold before us.

Two great armies were engaging just outside Jerusalem in the Valley of Megiddo.[26] The battle already raged as they fought against one another. As

---

25 Revelation 19:11-16
26 Revelation 19:19

we got closer to the earth, the participants in the battle became aware of our presence. As they did, they turned their attention from fighting each other, and began to direct their weapons at this newly perceived threat. Anti-aircraft weapons, tanks, rocket launchers and other weapons of human warfare were fired in our direction – all to no avail. Before they could ever reach us, the various projectiles were all vaporized by the pulsating waves of energy emanating from Christ.

As we sped closer and closer, I was able to actually see into the faces of the earthly combatants. Shock and panic were evident. Some were literally paralyzed with fear. In the face of many, however, was nothing less than demonic rage. It was then I became aware that in addition to the earthly combatants, there were indeed spiritual beings. Battling alongside the human soldiers were the forces of hell – demons, the fallen ones. Those who had once before raised their swords against God Himself were now battling again.

The human armies were no match for the power of Christ. As He opened His mouth and spoke, the power of His very words overwhelmed them.[27] I remembered seeing depictions of the blast of a nuclear weapon. The force of it would resonate over miles, vaporizing and obliterating everything in its path. I had thought that to be a powerful force – until I saw the force of His Word. The destruction was devastating. The two

---

[27] Revelation 19:15

hundred million soldiers who had come to battle were defeated in an instant. The blood from their bodies ran down the hills in streams until they reached the valley below, forming a river of blood that flowed four and five feet deep in places.[28]

The demonic forces continued to battle the angelic hosts until one by one they were defeated and each flung skyward into a distant star – the lake of fire.[29]

Then there remained only two – the man of sin and his accomplice, the false prophet. The false prophet had already fallen to his knees, whimpering, calling out for mercy. But the day of mercy had passed. He, too, was cast into the great burning lake.

The antichrist refused to bow. Belligerent, defiant, it appeared he would resist until the end. Then Christ approached and spoke directly to him, "Come out of him!" His face and body contorted as the power within him wrestled with the command of the Lord.

"COME OUT OF HIM!!"

The voice of the Lord thundered and reverberated across the valley and echoed in the mountains.

With a piercing shriek, the body of the antichrist yielded Lucifer himself - a writhing, hissing serpent form with eyes that were like glowing embers. Before Satan

---

28 Revelation 14:20
29 Revelation 19:20

could escape, he was captured by the pulsating energy of Christ. As he was held in the grip of Christ's power, angels proceeded to bind him with chains forged of the energy field itself. When he was secured, the earth opened beneath him and he was swallowed up. I heard the echo of his screams until the earth closed again to seal him in his prison for his 1,000-year sentence.[30]

No longer energized by Satan, the antichrist had himself fallen to his knees. I remembered the promise: *"Every knee shall bow...every tongue shall confess that Jesus Christ is Lord."*[31] And indeed, he did. But it was too late for him as well. He was cast into the same fire as the others before him.

As suddenly as it had begun, it was over. Every last vestige of resistance had been erased. Hosts of angels were dispatched to summon the remaining saints to gather for their introduction into the kingdom.[32] The remaining nations were gathered for their time of judgment. Christ reviewed each individual.[33] It was done in the same manner as the Judgment Seat had been done. Each individual felt as if their judgment was an individual one-on-one with Christ, yet they all occurred simultaneously.

---

[30] Revelation 20:1-3
[31] Philippians 2:9-11
[32] Matthew 24:31; Mark 13:27
[33] Matthew 25:32-46

The actions of each were reviewed, specifically how they had responded during the time of tribulation. Had they been compassionate and caring for those who were going through great troubles, or had they selfishly sought their own welfare and advancement during these times? Their actions were a reflection of their hearts, and even more so a reflection of their belief or lack of belief in the message that had been proclaimed by the 144,000[34] that had been used during the tribulation to carry the message of the grace of God.

Those who had accepted and believed the word of the witnesses heard the gracious voice of Christ. "You are blessed to enter the Kingdom prepared for you from the foundation of the world."

Their bodies were transformed. They were not the same as the glorified bodies of the church – and they did not have the supernatural abilities possessed by us. Nevertheless, they were dramatically changed. Every element of weakness and debilitation was instantly gone. Every element of the curse was eliminated. Their bodies reverted to the original design in the Garden, before sin was introduced.

But to the others, the word was one of judgment and rejection - "Depart!"

---

[34]Revelation 7:3-4

As the word was uttered, they were instantly transported to hell, there to await the day of the Great White Throne Judgment.

Once the judgment was completed, the whole earth seemed to take on a new appearance. It was similar to the earthly experience of a spring shower washing the pollen and pollutants out of the air, leaving a feeling of freshness and new life – only on a much greater scale. A wave of holy refreshing flowed from Christ in every direction, recapturing the beauty and wonder of a world that He had created – a creation that had caused Him to evaluate it as "very good."[35]

Thorns and weeds literally evaporated as the wave engulfed them, replaced by beautiful flowers and trees such as I had never seen.[36] Colors were more vibrant, some of them actually seeming to pulsate with a life of their own. The air had a fragrance about it that was both calming and exhilarating at the same time.

And so it had begun. We had entered the next phase of the plan of God – the one thousand year reign of Christ on the earth.

The voice of Christ thundered through the whole earth.

"Rejoice!!"

---

[35] Genesis 1:31
[36] Isaiah 35:1-2

CHAPTER 1

At Christ's word, Aleph sprang into action – he and a hundred million more just like him. Almost instantly tables appeared – hundreds of thousands of them, already loaded with food and beverage. I would try to describe them, but I could not. Not only were the food items unlike anything I had ever seen, but every table seemed to be unique. How was this even possible? How could there be that many varieties of food? But of course, God is infinite - infinite in His creativity, infinite in His imagination. We had gotten a glimpse of this in the millions of varied species of animals and plants that we had witnessed on earth. This was just another example.

Christ had chosen to manifest Himself in the physical form in which He had walked the earth some 2,000 years earlier. I was reminded of Aleph's words that the essence of a person does not change regardless of physical appearance. I and the rest of the body of Christ followed His lead, assuming a physical form that would allow us to interact with the others who had been called to the Marriage Supper of the Lamb.[37]

Christ spoke, and as He did, there was no sense of distance. Regardless of which of the hundreds of thousands of tables you were seated at, you felt as if you were in His immediate presence. All could see Him

---

[37] Revelation 19:7-9

equally well. All heard Him as if they were seated right next to Him.

He smiled. As He did, He raised His cup.

"Remember My promise. I told you that there would come a day when we would feast together in the Father's Kingdom.[38] The day has come! Today is the first day of the earthly manifestation of the rule of God!"

Thunderous applause and shouts of praise shook the ground so that it trembled as if we were having an earthquake.

"The kingdoms of this world are become the kingdoms of our God!"

Wave after wave of deafening praise! When it finally subsided, Christ continued.

"You are here as recipients of My grace, and the objects of My love. You will experience over the next 1,000 years[39] the great plan that prompted the creation of the universe. Unimaginable wonders await you. For now, enjoy the bounty that has been prepared for you. Take advantage of the opportunity to renew friendships and relationships with loved ones – and to become acquainted with others of whom you have only read or heard."

---

[38] Matthew 26:29
[39] Revelation 20:4-6

At these words, I became aware of the presence of saints of old, and personages of bygone ages. Adam, Moses, Abraham, Noah, Isaiah, Ruth, Esther, the apostles, Paul, Timothy, Mary – they were all there. In addition, the saints of all the previous ages were present – men and women that I had read about, and read their writings. Charles Spurgeon, Dwight Moody, Corrie Tin Boon, Martin Luther, Jonathan Edwards, Fanny Crosby, Billy Sunday, Oswald Chambers, A. W. Tozer and on and on and on.

Those who had been saved during the tribulation period were all there, along with those of the redeemed nation of Israel. This was quite the reunion. For the first time ever the entire assemblage of the believers of all ages were together. It would take some time to connect with them all – and it would certainly not be accomplished today. But there were many days to come.

For now, we would begin with those seated nearby us, as we all prepared to enjoy both the bounty from the table and the beginnings of relationships that would develop over the next millennium.

As Christ raised His cup to signal the beginning of the feast, we responded. The voice of Christ once more echoed throughout the earth. "Let the celebration begin!"

Each table seated a hundred or more. Families were grouped together, sometimes going back generations. As I looked around the table, I saw my wife, Jessica, seated next to me. Next to her were her own mother and father, Susan and John, who had been devout Christians and such a positive influence in our lives.

John's life had not started well. Both his parents were killed in an automobile accident when he was just an infant. He had been raised by foster parents. Fortunately, they had enough concern for his spiritual welfare to see that he was raised in church. He had accepted Christ at an early age while attending Vacation Bible School. Ironically, his foster parents never accepted Christ personally, and were not present to enjoy this reunion. They had attended church all their lives and been involved in many ministries. However their commitment had been to the church – not to Christ.

My own parents, Bob and Carolyn, were also seated around the table, along with both my grandmothers and one of my grandfathers. My dad had been raised as a Catholic, but became disheartened by what he saw as hypocrisy in the church. He met my mom when he was stationed at Fort Bragg, North Carolina while in the army. She was working at the local USO. They had fallen in love and married before either one of them became believers. They were both saved as a result of a visit by someone from a church in their community that was involved in Evangelism Explosion.

My parents had both been extremely influential in my life as a Christian. I was saved at a young age and was raised feeling like the church family was part of my extended family. Mom and Dad were thrilled when I announced that God had called me into the ministry.

There was our son, Brad, and his wife, Andria, and our precious twin grandchildren, Hart and Grace. They still appeared to me as they did when I had last seen them – four years old; Hart looking just like his dad, and Grace with her mother's beauty and mesmerizing smile! They had not been given glorified bodies at the time of the translation. That was reserved for those who had trusted Christ as Savior. They would grow up in the environment of the Kingdom.

Andria was a first generation Christian, and I was saddened, though not surprised, that I did not see any of her family in our assembly. A sadness accompanied each realization that some family members had not made it. They were not prepared when Christ returned. My own grandfather, who had died before I was even born. Andria's family, so resolute in their rejection of anything spiritual.

Our daughter, Julie had taken her seat next to Brad and Andria. Her husband, Roger, was among the missing. Julie and I had witnessed to him so many times, and there were times when I believed he was close to accepting Christ. He had even made a profession of faith early on in their relationship, but we both came to believe it was only because Julie would not date a non-Christian. In the end, his main concern was advancing his career and making money. He could never seem to see past the temporal to grasp the eternal. Many others were noticeable by their absence. While there was a sense of sadness, there was also a new understanding of God's grace and mercy. They had each had opportunities to accept the offer of salvation. Their rejection had resulted in their being excluded from this celebration.

In addition to family members, each table had members of the aforementioned groups of Saints of all the ages. Seated at the same table as my family were Barnabas[40] – the encourager – and several members of the early church whom he had led to Christ. It was such an honor to be in the presence of one who had been so instrumental in the spread of the gospel in the early days of the church.

Conversations turned toward reminiscing about the earthly relationships we had enjoyed together, and the expectations of what lie ahead. It would be redundant to attempt to record the repeated expressions of amazement and wonder. Repeatedly I heard phrases such as, "I never in my wildest dreams imagined it would be like this" and, "The beauty and splendor are almost overwhelming." The beauties could

---

[40] Acts 4:36

never even be conveyed in earthly language. There were no words in any earthly vocabulary to describe it.

We began to partake of the feast that was set before us. There was a plate of something that resembled grapes, but they had a unique consistency that was exhilarating when you bit into it. Other plates yielded wide varieties of unique tastes, each spectacular in its own way.

"Dad, you've got to try this!"

It was Brad, seated nearby to my right. As I turned toward him, I felt another wave of emotion. His appearance reflected what he had looked like as a teenager. The enthusiasm in his eyes, the huge smile on his face, instantly transported me back in time to those days on earth.

"What is it, son? What does it taste like?"

"That's just it," he said excitedly. "It tastes like anything! Take a bite and think of something – anything – and it immediately takes on the taste and texture of what you're thinking of."

I tried it. It was true! One bite was pepperoni pizza; the next was pecan pie, and then Jessica's wonderful chili. You could literally taste anything you could imagine from that one dish. We laughed and laughed as we each tried to come up with different tastes to try. Each one had its own memory of times on earth when we had enjoyed that dish together. The twins were delighted to feast on ice cream sundaes and sugar cookies.

We were back in time, that is, back in a place where time was a factor. I was aware that the sun had risen and set several times while we were feasting. The radiance that shown from Christ was so great that you really were not aware of any change in the light even after the sun had set. After many days, Christ stood once again.

"This time is coming to a close. But this is only the beginning. This was the start of the age of the reign of God on earth."

The shouts erupted again. "Hallelujah! Hallelujah! The kingdoms of this world are become the kingdoms of our God!"

After moments of praise, Christ raised His hand and we silenced our praise to hear what He would say.

"My kingdom will be one of righteousness and peace. It will also be one of justice and order."[41]

At that moment, two figures stepped up to stand on either side of Christ. It was Abraham and David. (I somehow just knew this, as did everyone else who saw them.)

Christ continued.

---

[41] Isaiah 11:1-5

"David[42] will govern over the twelve apostles,[43] who will rule over the twelve tribes of Israel in the land that was promised to Abraham – all the land between the Nile River and the Euphrates.[44] Areas have been appointed to each of them according to the lands given to each of Jacob's sons when they first entered the Promised Land.

"Furthermore, the remainder of the earth has been apportioned to them. The apostles will appoint judges over territories and individual cities. These judges will be appointed out of those who constitute My bride, the church. As promised, you will reign with Me during this thousand-year period of the kingdom of God on earth.[45] You have all already met your angelic guides. They will give you additional instructions on preparing to assume your new responsibilities.

"You have prayed for this day every time you repeated these words, 'Thy kingdom come, Thy will be done, on earth as it is in Heaven.'[46] The day has arrived!"

---

[42] II Samuel 7:16
[43] Matthew 19:28
[44] Deuteronomy 11:24; Joshua 1:3-4
[45] Revelation 20:6
[46] Matthew 6:10

CHAPTER 2

As Christ disappeared, so did the feasting tables. We now found ourselves grouped together in groups of a thousand. This was the number for which each angel guide was responsible. We would later learn that there were five million such groups, for the total number of the church approached five billion. Seems like a large number, until you realize it only represents about 3% of the people who lived during the 2,000 years from the formation of the church on the day of Pentecost until the rapture. *"Straight is the gate, and narrow is the way that leads to life, and few there be that find it."*[47]

Aleph had begun communicating.

"As our Master has said, His kingdom will be one characterized by order. You are part of the Matthew group. He is over the geographic area that you knew as South America. There are some 4,000,000 saints who will assist in the governing of the area. There will be five different areas of responsibility, all of which will be viewed as equally valuable and important. There are no insignificant roles in the kingdom.

"The five areas of responsibility are worship, agriculture, technology, construction and administrative. You will each have periods of time in each area of responsibility over the course of the

---

[47] Matthew 7:14

thousand years. There will be periods of time during which you will have no direct responsibilities. These will be times for you to explore the wonders of the world that is being transformed around you."

All of this information was somewhat overwhelming, yet there was still a sense of calm and confidence that I can only attribute to the transformation of my mind and consciousness to a supernatural level.

Aleph had continued. "You will find that the focus and priorities will change as the Kingdom Age unfolds. The early decades will focus on organization, construction and agriculture. Systems will have to be put into place to provide housing and food for the population. Worship will always be a priority. The worship teams will organize local worship opportunities, as well as coordinate the visits to Jerusalem for the annual Feast of Tabernacles.

"As you progress through the millennial, situations and circumstances will evolve. The population of the earth right now is the smallest it will be. The mortals who live during the Age will bear children, and since there will be no death, the population will increase exponentially. The other major change will revolve around the submission to the reign of Christ. Everyone on the earth right now has already committed to the Lordship of Christ. As the children are born and mature, they will have the opportunity to make that choice for themselves. As a result, as we get into the later stages of the Age, there will be some who might resist the authority of Christ, and you as His representatives."

This was difficult to comprehend. I had not even thought about that possibility. Here we were in a perfect environment, in a world that would know no disease, no injustice, no crime. Who would want to change anything?

Aleph was continuing his discourse. "Of course, the enemy is bound. There will be no influence from him or any of his minions. There will also be none of the negative influences that lured many of the young and old alike during your time on earth. Nevertheless, there is an element within some that resist authority and reject all restriction. In the later years of the Age, there will be more need for oversight and exercise of judgment. The Word of Christ will be the ultimate source of law. There will be more individual instruction later. For now, absorb the enormity of the opportunities that await you."

It was indeed a lot to absorb. Smaller groups formed as families and acquaintances, new and old, began to share thoughts about the different areas of service and how the various responsibilities would be carried out. Aleph was making his way from group to group, answering questions. At some of the groups, we would hear shouts of excitement, but we chose not to infringe on their celebration. We continued talking until he appeared to the group that my family and I were in.

"Any questions?" he asked.

There were several questions about the different ministries. Then I raised a question about those who would be born, the population increase to which he had referred.

"Are these newly created souls that are being born?"

"No," Aleph responded. "These newly born are the souls of those who died on earth before reaching an age of accountability, before they were able to choose between good and evil. They include the hundreds of millions of unborn who were aborted before they had an opportunity to be born. They will be born into the families of the earth, be raised in the perfect environment of the Age, and have the privilege to choose to be a part of the Kingdom of Messiah."

Aleph now turned specifically to Jessica and me.

"I have another surprise for you."

At this moment, another angel appeared next to Aleph. He was holding an infant. He passed the child to Aleph, and then disappeared.

Aleph turned to us and said, "This is your daughter. Jessica, you lost a child through miscarriage. She has been here waiting for you. She is yours to love, to raise during the Age." With this, he passed the child into my wife's arms.

I had thought there could be no greater exhilaration than I had already felt – but this surpassed anything I had experienced. We literally trembled with excitement as we held our new daughter. Family and friends gathered around, as they would have at the hospital nursery. She was beautiful – truly radiant. I now understood the shouts of excitement we had heard from the other groups. We were not the only ones being reunited with members of the family we had never met.

"What shall we call her?" I asked.

"She has always been Elizabeth to me," Jessica said.

"Elizabeth it is," I said. This thrilled Jessica's mom, who was standing nearby with the family. Elizabeth was her middle name. We laughed and cried and took turns holding Elizabeth for many, many hours.

Aleph had slipped away to meet with other groups, but now reappeared. He addressed Jessica and me.

"You will not have any other responsibilities for the first two hundred years, other than raising your child. The progress of time and aging will be slowed to what it was prior to the flood of Noah's day.[48] One hundred years will be the same as approximately ten earth years, so that at the end of two hundred years, Elizabeth will be the equivalent of twenty years old. This will give you much more time to enjoy each part of her

---

[48] Isaiah 65:20

childhood, and also give you greater opportunity to instruct and guide her in the ways of the Kingdom. Remember that one day she will have to exercise her will to choose to follow Christ."

"Well, of course, she will," I thought. I could imagine no other outcome. Of course she would choose to follow Christ.

I looked at that precious face and made a silent vow within myself:

"You will choose to follow Christ. I will make sure of it."

CHAPTER 3

There were several days of excited activity as we attempted to acclimate ourselves to our new environment. Aleph met with everyone individually to discuss his or her responsibilities during the opening years of the Kingdom. Positions were assigned according to the individuals' own personalities, all of which Aleph was intimately acquainted with.

Aleph had already told Jessica and me that we would have no primary responsibilities during the early years of Elizabeth's life. In addition to raising and enjoying her, we would be able to participate in any of the different areas of ministry to whatever extent we chose.

Brad, Andria and Julie had all been assigned to one of the praise teams. No wonder there, the way they had all been so involved in the music programs of their church. My parents, Bob and Carolyn, were part of one of the agriculture teams. Again, no shock. They had always loved gardening and working outside. Dad had grown up on a farm and had always expressed a desire to "go back to his roots" – and, yes, he did indeed mean it as a pun. Jessica's parents, John and Susan would start out on one of the construction teams.

I was standing outside enjoying the scenery when two eagles soaring in the distance caught my eye. As unusual as it was to see two of them flying in tandem, that was not what drew my attention to them. Aleph had said that no matter the physical form, we would still be able to recognize each other. I watched as they circled nearer and nearer, until they both landed directly in front of me. That is when they reassumed their human forms.

"Brad, Andria, good to see you. That was some entrance."

"I've always wanted to do that," said Brad. "That was exhilarating!"

"I'll say," said Andria. "That was an excellent idea. I used to have dreams about being able to fly, but it was not nearly as exciting as the real thing."

"Where's Julie?" I asked.

Brad answered, "She's with Hart and Grace. They were napping and Julie said she would stay with them. Where are Mom and Lizzie?"

(Brad's pet name for Elizabeth had stuck. She was now Lizzie to everyone.)

"They're down by the stream," I said. "Let's join them."

Closing our eyes and thinking of where we wanted to be was all it took to be standing beside them.

Jessica's eyes lit up. "Hello! So good to see you both. Hugs all around!"

"Where's Lizzie?" Andria asked.

"She's sleeping."

Our eyes followed Jessica's as she looked behind us. There was Lizzie, sleeping peacefully – in the curled up arm of a sleeping lion![49] There was a moment of startled shock, followed by an eruption of laughter from everyone. This new world of peace and tranquility was going to take some getting used to.

We sat down, and I turned back to Brad and Andria. "I understand you two are on the worship teams. How's that going?"

They both began talking at once, obviously very excited. "Whoa, whoa! One at a time," I said.

Brad grinned and bowed to Andria, deferring to her to begin. She playfully punched him in the shoulder, but still took advantage of the opportunity to share first.

"It is unbelievable. The groups are huge – several thousand in each – and of course, everyone's voice is amazing! I've never heard such harmonies."

Brad had restrained himself as long as he could. "At first everyone is just singing, praising. It was like one gigantic worship service. After a while, we began to

---

[49] Isaiah 11:6-8

discuss our role in the Kingdom. We obviously knew that praise and worship would be a central focus, but we did not know what that would actually look like.

"We chose to divide into three different groups. One would form smaller groups- literally tens of thousands of groups - that would travel over our area and even into other parts of the globe, with the idea that there would be constant praise. Somewhere in our area, at all times, someone would be praising. Some of the groups have already begun. It's so awesome to see people gather from all directions to listen or to join in."

"I've already heard some of them!" Jessica exclaimed. "What a blessing! To just be strolling along outside and hear the sound of music as if it were coming from the sky itself. Heavenly, truly heavenly."

"The second group will prepare worship for our Sabbath meetings," Andria inserted. "Every region will have their own times of praise and worship every week, and these teams will lead in that worship. Brad, Julie and I are on one of these teams. I've heard that Christ Himself will appear from time to time at the regional worship meetings. How exciting will that be?"

Brad picked up from there. "The third team will prepare for the annual trip to Jerusalem for the celebration of Feast of Tabernacles.[50] With each region having a part of the worship ministry committed to that

---

[50] Zechariah 14:16

preparation, I cannot even imagine how majestic that is going to be. And there is so much talent and creativity! I don't want to spoil the surprises, but there were some unbelievable ideas that were floated regarding new avenues of worship."

"And we will all rotate so that everyone gets to be a part of each of the groups," Andria added.

"Sounds amazing," I said. "Have you talked to any of the rest of the family?"

"Not recently," Brad said. "I'd love to hear about how things are going in the other ministry departments."

"Well," Jessica said, "why not contact them?"

All we had to do was to think about our desire to communicate with them, and within a few moments, there they were. Greetings and hugs were exchanged again.

"Brad and Andrea were just updating us on the progress of the praise teams," I said. "How are things going in the other ministries?"

John opened the conversation. "The construction project is an enormous challenge. When you realize that so much of the earth was devastated by the events of the tribulation, it is a tremendous task just to clear away the debris in many areas. Then there are hundreds of millions with no home. Of course, it's not exactly the crisis of the homeless that we knew when we lived here before. The elements are not a challenge. You could literally live outdoors all the time if you chose to do so. But we have been charged with the initial responsibility of building dwellings."

Susan chimed in here. "We are starting with some single family housing, but some of the groups in some areas are already discussing doing some high-rises and other multi-family housing. Of course, not all the construction is from the ground up. There are buildings that are still standing from the tribulation period that just need to be repaired, renovated and inspected for soundness. We can use those until new construction replaces them."

"What are you using for tools? Where are you getting materials?" Brad asked.

"Well, for starters," John said, "not all the factories were completely destroyed. And there are plenty of raw materials. Equipment that may have been designed for other purposes is being converted to use in construction. Remember what Isaiah and Micah said about beating swords into plowshares and spears into pruning hooks?[51] We're able to utilize some of the items left behind in our construction projects."

Bob and Carolyn had been listening, trying to absorb all this new information just like the rest of us.

---

[51] Isaiah 2:4; Micah 4:3

Mary turned to them and asked about the agricultural teams.

"Oh, I don't even know where to begin," Bob said. "The early stages of this will be pretty simple, believe it or not. With the curse lifted from the earth, growing things is not a problem at all. For that matter, just the items growing in the wild would be more than enough to sustain life. Initially we'll concentrate on designating areas for crop growth and devising means of distribution.

"But there is already talk of cultivating new strains of fruits and vegetables by cross-pollinating. With groups all over the world focusing on growing the best and most innovative crops, you'll have a constantly evolving array of tastes and treats. And with the earth's environment being freed from the curse, there is no more need for pesticides or any chemical additives. Everything produced will be perfectly healthy. You can eat anything you want, as much as you want, with no negative side effects."

He was positively beaming!

Carolyn brought up an entirely different perspective. "One of the challenges right now is to change the mindset of those left over from the pre-Kingdom age. Nothing will be bought or sold. Everything is produced for the enjoyment of everyone else. It will take a while for some to get accustomed to a new economy, where the goal is not profit or personal enrichment, but production for the glory of Christ and for the edification of all."

There was that somewhat sobering reality again. Not everyone was in glorified bodies. Not all minds had been converted to spiritual thinking. In the midst of this utopian existence, there would be future challenges.

We heard Lizzie as she began to wake up. The lioness waited patiently until Jessica came over to retrieve her, then rose, licked Jessica's hand, and ambled off into the nearby grove of trees. There was the customary cooing and baby talk as everyone took turns interacting with Lizzie. She had her mother's beauty and an inner joy that radiated from her face.

After several minutes of conversation, John motioned for me to move with him away from the rest of the family. As we walked along the edge of the stream, he began talking in a more serious tone.

"What did Aleph mean when he said what he did about Elizabeth having to make a choice to follow Christ? Isn't the fact that she is your and Jessica's child enough?"

"I guess not. And I understand. She has not had the opportunity to willingly give her heart to Christ. Our Lord never forced anyone to accept Him, or to serve Him – or to love Him. There will come a time when she will make that choice."

"But does that mean there will be some who will choose not to accept? There is no way my granddaughter will reject Christ! I won't allow it!"

I had to smile a little, even while discussing such a serious subject. I guess grandparents are grandparents, no matter the dispensation.

"I couldn't agree more," I said. "We have several decades to instill in her a love for Christ. She will see His love shown both in our love for her, and in all the marvelous blessings He has given us. When the time comes, she will respond in love to Him. Come on – let's join the others. It's almost time for dinner!"

After we had eaten and smaller groups formed for conversation, my thoughts turned to Julie. I had not had much opportunity to interact with her since the Marriage Supper, and I felt the need to talk. Plus, any excuse to see my grandchildren was always welcome! Closing my eyes, I transported to where Julie was.

She was sitting in a park area that Brad and Andria had designed and built for the children. Complete with swings and slides as well as some interactive activity areas, it was obviously a place that Grace and Hart would enjoy for years. It still took a little getting used to when I thought about the slow aging process. The grandchildren would be infants for another couple of decades, then gradually age into what we had called teenagers by the close of the first century of the

Kingdom. That was fine by me. I was looking forward to enjoying every moment of their lives.

Julie had been pushing the children on the swings when I materialized.

Her face lit up just the way it always had when I would get home. "Hi, Daddy!" she squealed. At that moment, she was six years old herself, running and jumping into my outstretched arms. As I caught her and held her to my chest, we were transported in our minds back to the days when we had developed our close relationship – when I was her hero and she was my princess. For several minutes – or was it hours? – we basked in the glow of the love of a father and his daughter.

Our attention then turned to Hart and Grace, and for the next several hours we were enraptured by their giggles and squeals as we played and cavorted, making up games and, of course, always letting the children win.

Finally, we wore them out and they fell asleep on the grass in the shade of a giant tree known as a Chile Pine. It was also referred to as a Monkey Puzzle. How appropriate for our little monkeys to fall asleep there!

As they slept, it gave an opportunity for Julie and me to have one of our father-daughter chats.

"We haven't had a lot of opportunities to talk."

"I know," Julie said, "and I've missed that. There's so much activity!"

"Yes, but I don't ever want to lose our closeness. We'll just have to make that a priority."

"Agreed!"

So we talked – about the Kingdom, about our memories of our earthly lives, about things we wanted to do and places we wanted to visit, about the future – even extending beyond the Kingdom Age.

"Do you think of Roger often?" I almost regretted bringing up the subject. For the first time in our conversation, there was a tinge of sadness.

"I do. I loved him – still do, I suppose, only with a different perspective. I wish he were here, wish he could experience and enjoy all that God has provided for us. Yet there's an understanding that he would not be totally happy here. He never submitted to the Lordship of Christ, and he would not accept His authority here. Unless a person has surrendered their will to Christ's will, there will always be a spirit of rebellion and resistance. Roger would have enjoyed the perfect environment, but would have still wanted to control his own life, to do things his way. As a result, he would never have been completely satisfied, and his dissatisfaction would have been a negative influence on everyone he came in contact with.

"I do miss him, but Christ has always been my first love, and His love has filled every void that might have been left by any loss."

I was amazed at the insight and wisdom of my little girl.

"You're as amazing as always. You were always my shining light. What do you say we wake up the kids and take them to see Grandma?"

CHAPTER 4

Time had taken on a new dimension, especially for those of us in glorified bodies. There was no need for sleep. There were times when Jessica and I would choose to "follow the sun." By moving around the world along with the earth's rotation, we could actually stay in perpetual daylight. But after stretches of 24 hour a day activity, it was good sometimes to just have periods of quiet and reflection. The best time for this was during the night hours when there was less activity.

Those not in glorified bodies still primarily utilized the nighttime hours to refresh and replenish their energy. However, even they had a new perspective of time. There wasn't the stress that many had lived under on the pre-Kingdom earth. The slowing of the aging process and the knowledge that there were ten centuries of life ahead contributed to a much more relaxed approach to living.

That is not to say there was not a lot going on. Each new day brought new opportunities to explore the creation. There were so many parts of the earth Jessica and I had never seen during our natural lives. Not that we would not have liked to, but there were so many restrictions. I had always worked, right up until the rapture, so the only time for travelling was during vacations. Then of course, there were always the financial considerations. We were never wealthy. (You did not get wealthy on a pastor's salary – at least not the pastors that I knew!) So when we did travel, it was usually a week or so at the beach, or maybe in the mountains. But we never travelled outside the United States, and only saw a small percentage of the attractions there.

So for the first few decades, we travelled. Sometimes we would take Lizzie with us. She was no trouble at all and of course, there were no safety concerns. Other times we would leave her with Brad and Andrea, or with Julie, or with one of the sets of grands, and we would travel alone.   It was on one of those occasions when we were traveling alone that we decided to go to Israel.

We had the ability to travel by way of "thought projection". We could travel anywhere on the earth by just visualizing where we wanted to be and willing ourselves to be there. However, there were other times when we chose to travel in a way as to allow us to enjoy the scenery along the way. On the trip to Israel, we had chosen the scenic route. We traveled all of the distance from our base in South America across the Atlantic Ocean by swimming.

Sounds crazy, doesn't it? Being able to assume whatever form we chose let us travel part of the way with a school of dolphins, and when we really wanted to cover some ground we would choose the form of great whales. In this form, we were able to cover over one hundred miles per day as we made the six thousand mile journey.

But we were in no particular hurry. As we made our way toward the Middle East – now known as Canaan – we took our time and explored the wonders of the sea. There were animals in the depths of the ocean resembling nothing that we had ever seen. In addition, the coral and rock formations were fascinating.

On one such jaunt into the depths, we journeyed into the Puerto Rico Trench. This is the deepest part of the Atlantic Ocean, located on the boundary between the Caribbean Sea and the Atlantic Ocean. It is 497 miles long and has a maximum depth of 28,373 feet, or a little over five miles at Milwaukee Deep, the deepest point in the trench. Humans had ventured here in deep water craft with cameras, but no one had ever experienced it in the way that Jessica and I were. The pressure at this depth is a crushing 16,000 pounds per square inch.

I'm not sure which was more amazing – that God had created creatures that had been able to survive these extreme conditions while we lived on earth, or that Jessica and I were swimming here as casually as if we were enjoying a dip in the family pool.

At one point, I looked over at Jessica, who had assumed the form of a mermaid! Not to be outdone, I assumed the form of Aquaman, the DC comic hero who lived under water. (Ironically, he was able to communicate telepathically with the sea creatures as well as withstand the tremendous pressures of deep ocean, just as we now could.) We cavorted and played for several hours before returning to the surface.

As we broke the surface of the water, Jessica was laughing out loud. (My, how I loved her laugh!)

"Aquaman? Seriously? What are you – thirteen?"

"I can be thirteen if I want! I can be anything I want! When I was a boy, I read comic books like most of the boys my age. We thrilled at the exploits of Aquaman, and Superman – even Thor, a supposed Norse god. And here we are with abilities and power that surpasses any of them! All of them put together, actually, since we can assume the form and ability of any of them at will."

We took some time out to praise God once again for providing such a magnificent existence for His children.

"Let's fly the rest of the way," Jessica suggested.

With that, Superman and Superwoman streaked across the sky toward Jerusalem.

In less than five seconds, we touched down on the shore of the Sea of Galilee. We arrived in Canaan as the preparations were being completed for the annual observance of the Feast of Tabernacles. We could attend the Feast as often as we liked, but everyone was required to attend at least once every one hundred years during the course of the Kingdom Age.

Of course, not everyone could attend the same year. The city could not contain that many people. Restrictions had to be placed on who could attend for the first one hundred years. Everyone was excited to be a part of the celebration, but the only ones who would be allowed to join the Jews during the earliest celebrations would be the church. We had not yet attended the Feast as participants, but were scheduled to do so in the next decade.

Not only were the numbers a problem, but those in their earthly bodies needed transportation. Unable to tele-transport as we were, they would have to have physical means of transportation. Inventive solutions were already being put into action, but the manufacture of the cars, trains, planes and other means of transportation would have to wait for the construction of the factories that would build them.

Touring the city of Jerusalem and the surrounding area brought back memories of the events of the Bible that had taken place on the very ground on which we were walking. We visited the Pool of Bethesda where the crippled man had been healed.[52] We walked out toward the Mount of Olives, where Jesus had been transfigured, from where He had ascended into Heaven,

---

[52] John 5:2-9

and to which He had returned.[53]   Of course, this had been changed dramatically by His return. As Zechariah had prophesied, the mountain had split into two great pieces when His feet touched on it.[54]   There were now two great hills separated by a three-mile wide valley.

The city itself was a bustle of activity. In addition to the preparation for the Feast, there was a tremendous amount of construction going on, in addition to the normal activities of the residents. The Jewish people had relocated to Canaan to reclaim their homeland and the promise made to Abraham and their ancestors.

The temple services had been reinstituted, but with a different perspective of course. There was no longer any need for sacrificial offerings, for there was no more sin among them. Their wills and beings had been submitted to the Person of Christ. They had all come to accept Him, not only as their long-awaited Messiah, but also as their Savior and Lord.   The services were all about praise and recognition of what Christ had accomplished in redeeming them as a people, delivering them from the bondage of sin, and faithfully fulfilling His promises made to their ancestors.

We made our way up to the top of the eastern ridge, along with several hundred other travelers. The Mount was a very popular attraction and always had myriads of visitors, made up of both glorified saints as

---

[53] Matthew 17:1-2; Acts 1:9-12
[54] Zechariah 14:4

well as those still in earthly bodies. As we neared the top, we noticed several groups clustered together in different spots along the side and face of the hill. We soon realized that these groups were gathered around individuals from the pages of Scripture.

"Oh, look," Jessica said. "There's Isaiah! And there's Timothy over with that group."

There was no problem recognizing them, even the ones with which we had not already had contact. There was that sense of recognition that allowed us to connect with anyone, whether we had physically met them or not.

"Look over here," I said, directing her attention toward a large group gathered over on a gentle slope. "That's Adam!"

For a few moments, I was literally speechless. That was the very first man, the one that the very hand of Jehovah had fashioned from the dust of the ground, the man into whom He had breathed the first breath of life.[55] We made our way over to the edge of the group to eavesdrop on the conversations taking place.

Adam was patiently answering the same questions he had already been asked hundreds of times since the beginning of the Kingdom Age.

"What were your first conscious thoughts?"

[55] Genesis 2:7

"How long were you in the Garden of Eden prior to the fall?"

"How could you have been so foolish as to be deceived by Satan?"

At this last question, Adam appeared to sadden.

"Every mortal has lived with regrets over choices and decisions they made. None, of course, had the far-reaching effects of my failure. My consolation in looking back is the realization that Jehovah was able to use my failure to demonstrate His mercy and great love in redeeming humanity from the sin that I allowed to be introduced into the world. His grace has also forgiven and restored me to His fellowship and favor. It is the source of my eternal devotion and love for Him."

It was a touching moment. I was also impressed by the fact that Adam made no mention of Eve's part in the fall. Unlike in the Garden when he had shifted the blame over to her,[56] he accepted full responsibility for his actions.

"That was a special moment." Jessica's comment brought me back to the present. I had been so absorbed with listening to Adam that I had lost awareness of where I was.

"Yes. I was thinking the same thing. Living here in this environment, in glorified bodies, makes it easy to

---

[56] Genesis 3:12

forget where we came from, and the price that was paid for us to be here."

Jessica looked at me, her eyes misty. "I want to go to Jesus."

Taking her hand and visualizing the Lord, we found ourselves instantly at the throne. At the center of the city, Jesus had established His throne. The seraphim were there continuously, even as John had seen them in the Revelation, constantly circling the throne. Their constant chant, "Holy, holy, holy, Lord God Almighty, which was, and is, and is to come"[57] was a never-ending affirmation of the identity and the character of the One who sat on the throne.[58]

He was as we had seen Him before – magnificent in His brilliant glory, awesome in His majesty. As we knelt before the throne, I again had that experience of intimacy. Although there were thousands gathered and bowed before Him – there were always thousands – there was a sense in which He connected with me personally. In that moment, it was as if everyone else disappeared and I knelt alone before Him.

I began to worship Him, extolling His greatness, His mercy, His love – every virtue I could call to mind. My praise was so much more pure than any I had been able to render on earth. I was unencumbered by any other thoughts, undistracted by any other activity. As I

[57] Revelation 4:8
[58] Isaiah 6:2-3

worshipped, His presence engulfed me and we became as one. At some point I remembered the prayer of Jesus when He was still on earth with His disciples – "...*that they all may be one; as Thou, Father art in Me, and I in Thee, that they also may be one in us...*"[59]

It was indescribable. My essence – given to me by the Source of all life – was now reconnected with that source. In that moment, I was one with the Divine. Time stood still. I was there for eternity – and yet just a moment.

"Rise, my son." He spoke to me.

I stood to my feet. I was back before the throne, Jessica at my side. Her face radiated with the glory of Christ. There was no doubt she had just experienced the same thing as I. We again bowed before Him, and instantly we were back on the outskirts of the city.

---

[59] John 17:21

CHAPTER 5

I took advantage of an opportunity to join John and Susan at one of the organizational meetings for the construction team with which they were involved. Shortly after the beginning of the Kingdom Age, they had to discuss how the projects would be organized. They stood along with several thousand others as the leader of their team explained the process.

Among this group were representatives from each of the different groups now living on earth:

- The angels were there, although unseen, existing now as they ever had, as servants to God and His creation.
- There were the Saints. These were those who made up the Church, the body of Christ, who had been transformed and given supernatural bodies at the time of the Rapture.
- Then there were the Adamites. These were the ones who had been redeemed and granted access into the Kingdom in the physical state that God had designed and created in the Garden of Eden, before the fall. This included the entire Jewish nation, with the exception of those who had been saved through faith in Christ during the church age. It also included the saints from the Old Testament and the tribulation saints, both the ones who had been martyred for their faith, and

the ones who endured until the end of the tribulation. The physical bodies of the Adamites were perfect, immensely capable and immortal, but lacked the supernatural capabilities of the Saints.

- In addition, there were the Mortals. These were those who had entered the Kingdom as children, and those who would be born during the Kingdom Age. They had the same physical bodies as the Adamites, but were not yet redeemed, and thus had not been given the gift of eternal life.

My own grandchildren, Hart and Grace, and my daughter, Lizzie, were Mortals. As they matured in the Kingdom, they would have to exercise their free will to choose to accept the Lordship of Christ and surrender their wills to Him. At that time, they would be given the gift of eternal life. Otherwise, they would be subject to the deception that would come at the end of the Kingdom Age.

The team leader had begun his explanation.

"The initial phase of the work had been to evaluate the buildings that survived the tribulation and Armageddon to determine whether it would be more efficient to try to modify them for their new purposes, or just to raze them and start from the ground up with all new structures. Over time, all the buildings will be replaced. The craftsmanship that was available at the time does not rival what is now available. Plus, all the factories will need to be retooled for the manufacture of new products."

One of the Adamites indicated he had a question. "What energy sources are available to us?"

"Going forward, all power will come from solar energy. We will utilize the energy sources that we have available for the time being, but the goal will be to have everything solar powered by the end of the first century."

"And what is required of us?" This from another of the Adamites. "We haven't been given any information as to schedules or responsibilities.

"Your responsibilities will initially be assigned according to the needs of the particular day. As you progress, you will have a great deal of freedom to move from project to project depending on your interests and initiative. As to your schedule, this will also be up to you. It will take a while to get accustomed to the new priorities of the Kingdom. We are under no time pressure, no profit pressure. The items that are produced will be available to any who desire them at no cost. The initiative to work and produce will come from the satisfaction of being involved in serving others and producing items that fill a need."

There was a murmur among the crowd as this information was absorbed and discussed.

Someone standing near John and Susan remarked, "I don't see how this is going to work. What is the motivation to work? Won't there be some who choose to just do nothing?"

John was the first to speak up. "The motivation will be one's own sense of accomplishment and usefulness. Sure, there will be some in the early years who will take advantage of the environment to enjoy travelling or 'doing nothing', and that is perfectly acceptable. But there is an innate desire in each person to be useful, to accomplish. Eventually this will bring everyone into the work force.

"There will also be an element of peer pressure that will be in play. When products start rolling off the line and people see the advantages of everyone working together, no one will want to be sitting on the sidelines. Not the least of the motivating factors will be the desire to please our Lord. All of our labor is ultimately an expression of our love for and devotion to Him."

Most were nodding their heads in agreement, although there were a few who seemed to have a "wait and see" attitude about this new philosophy. It was to be expected. It was radically different from anything they had ever been exposed to during their earthly existence.

After a few more minutes of discussion, the leader of the group resumed his presentation.

"There are tens of thousands of groups meeting around the world just as we are. Initially our focus will be on providing for the needs of our immediate area – housing, roadways, transportation, energy sources, distribution facilities, etc. Over time, we will turn our attention to producing products for distribution worldwide.

"The opportunities for creativity and ingenuity will be unlimited. As I stated earlier, nothing will be bought or sold, so the challenge will be to create and deliver products that have broad appeal. The more the demand for the products that we will produce in our sector, the greater will be the satisfaction in our accomplishment. In other words, the greater our service to the overall good, the greater the reward."

"As it should be," Susan thought. "He who would be great in the Kingdom of God must be the servant of all."[60]

"And so, if there are no further questions, it's time to get started. Each of you has been assigned to smaller groups and initial areas of focus. Report to your individual team leaders, and may the blessings of the Lord be on you!"

---

[60] Mark 10:43-44

****

Fifty years had passed since that first meeting. Enormous progress had been made since that initial introduction to the new order. The basic needs of housing, energy and transportation had been met during the first decade. Attention had then turned to innovation. As John had predicted, there was a sense of excitement and accomplishment that drew everyone into the work force.

At one of our family get-togethers, it was obvious that John and Susan were excited about their latest project.

"It's beyond amazing," John said. "The level of creativity is off the charts. You would expect that the glorified Saints would possess extraordinary abilities of invention – and that is true – but the abilities of many of the Adamites to understand and relate to the products and services that will appeal to the masses of humanity have also been extremely impressive."

"So true," Susan said. "Our current project is in the transportation field. Without the ability to tele-transport, travel has been somewhat restricted for the Adamites. The project we are working on now is a hovercraft that utilizes electro-magnetic fields as its power source. The fields themselves will be solar powered, so it will have unlimited range. As long as you have access to the sun, it will operate indefinitely."

"Wow!" was Brad's reaction. "How about the speed?"

Everyone laughed. It was no surprise that Brad's first concern would be how fast it would go.

"Oh, great," I said. "Now I have to be worried about speeding tickets...again!"

This brought another wave of laughter.

"Fortunately, that will not be a concern," John said. "Not that it won't be fast. The prototypes have already reached speeds of 500 miles per hour, and the expectation is that they will ultimately be able to achieve Mach 1 – approximately 760 miles per hour at sea level. But the safety features of both the hover craft and the highways will mean that accidents will be impossible, therefore there will be no need for speed control."

"However," Susan added emphatically, "we have decided," cutting her eyes toward John as she continued, "to have a regulator that limits the top end to just under Mach 1 to avoid the sound clutter associated with constantly breaking the sound barrier."

"Yes," John said, smiling. "That was a unanimous decision."

We all laughed again. Some things never change.

CHAPTER 6

Seventy years into the Kingdom Age, the time was approaching for our trip to Jerusalem for the Feast of Tabernacles. As we prepared for our trip, it was a good opportunity to review with the children the significance of the feasts. After family dinner one Monday evening, we all gathered into the living room. Grace and Hart, now the equivalent of eleven earth years, and Lizzie, seven, sat down in the center of the floor with the grown-ups seated in a circle.

"Ok, everyone, it's test time."

"All right," Grace said, "let's do it."

We had done this so many times that it wasn't really a challenge. It was more an opportunity for the kids to show off. I also knew that every opportunity to reinforce the information and the principles would serve them well later, both in their own lives and as they shared them with their children. It was the same concept that God had introduced to the Israelites to communicate His ways to their descendents.

"Ok, first question. Where do we find the description of the annual feasts all in one chapter in the Bible?"

Grace's hand shot up, and before I could even point to her she blurted out, "Leviticus 23!"

"That's right," I said. "But wait until I point to you – give everyone a chance. Now how many feasts are described there?"

All three hands shot up almost simultaneously.

"Let's let Lizzie handle this one," I said.

She looked around the room and smiled at everyone and began, "There are seven feasts altogether. Four spring feasts and three fall..."

"Hold on, hold on," I interrupted. "You're getting ahead of me."

"Well," she said, "I already know what the next question is going to be. It will be the number of spring feasts and fall feasts, and there are four spring feasts and three fall feasts."

"You are absolutely right. But from now on, wait until I ask the question. You do want my participation, right? Now, the questions get a little tougher. What are the four spring feasts? I believe it's Hart's turn."

As he counted off one, two, three, four on his fingers, Hart said, "Passover, Unleavened Bread, First Fruits, Pentecost. Dad, we've been over these, like a thousand times."

"We have, son. And we'll probably go over them ten thousand more times. They have tremendous significance for all of us – not just for the Jews. In fact, that brings us to the next question.   What is the significance of the three spring feasts?"

Again, Grace's hand shot up.

"The three spring feasts are pictures of Yeshua's first coming, when He came as a Baby in Bethlehem. The Passover is the offering of His blood for our sins, so that we could be passed over in the day of judgment, just as He passed over the houses in Egypt when He brought the last plague on Pharaoh.[61]   The Feast of Unleavened Bread was the offering of His perfect body and blood, and His burial. The Feast of Firstfruits – this is my favorite – is when He arose from the grave."

As she said, "arose from the grave," she added her own theatrics, rising up from the floor with a victorious flourish.

"Correct…", I started.

"Annnnnd," she interrupted with a wag of her finger, "Pentecost is the coming of the Holy Spirit and the birth of the church."

With that, she crossed her arms emphatically and resumed her seat on the floor.

"Very good.   Now, what about the Fall Feasts. Lizzie? Care to try those?"

---

[61] Exodus 12:12-13

"Of course, Dad. They're easy. The fall feasts are all about the second coming of Christ, when He returned after the Tribulation. There's the Feast of Trumpets, the Day of Atonement and the Feast of Tabernacles."

"And what about their Hebrew names? Hart?"

"Rosh Hashanah, Yom Kippur and Succoth."

"Very good. Now what about the meanings of the fall feasts?"

Grace was ready again. "The Feast of Trumpets is the sign of a new beginning, the beginning of the rule of Yeshua on the earth. The Day of Atonement speaks of sin forever being put away during His righteous rule. The Feast of Tabernacles is a funny one. The Jews all have to live in tents or huts for a week to remind them of the time they wandered in the wilderness."[62]

"Excellent," I said. "And remember it's because they doubted the promise of God when they first came to the Jordan River to cross into Canaan, that they were forced to wander in the wilderness, living in tents and temporary dwellings, until that entire generation died."[63]

The other adults had been listening appreciatively, but with this last bit of information, Julie spoke up.

---

[62] Leviticus 23:42-43
[63] Numbers 13, 14

"I've heard a rumor that there is an application of that same concept that will be incorporated into our observance of the Feast, but no one is talking about the details. The ones who have attended the Feast in previous years never speak of their time here in Jerusalem. I'm excited, and more than a little curious."

"So what do you think?" Brad asked. "Do you have any idea what the big secret is?"

"No," I answered. "I really don't. I've thought a lot about it. The observance by the Jews was to remind them of what they had been delivered from. Living in a tent or a hut would not have the same significance to us as it did to them, because they actually lived in those during their sojourn in the wilderness."

"I just think it's a little strange that no one ever discusses their time here," Jessica said. "There must be a reason why Christ wants to surprise us with whatever awaits us."

****

Two weeks later, we were in Jerusalem for the observance of Succoth. We had left the children with friends rather than bringing them on this particular trip.

"I've heard more rumors," Susan said.

All attention turned to her. "Rumors of what?" we all asked almost simultaneously.

"Just rumors," she said, with that sly smile that we remembered from our earthly existence. "And if they are true, then we are in for a most interesting week."

Just then, Aleph appeared.

"Hello, old friend," I said. "We haven't seen too much of you lately."

"You've been doing very well on your own. Plus there are other responsibilities that occupy me."

I was curious about what those other responsibilities might be, but before we could begin that conversation, Aleph had moved on to his current mission.

"I'm here to share with you concerning your observance of Succoth. Since this is your first time here for the Feast of Tabernacles, you must be made aware of the procedures. You are all familiar with how the Jewish people have observed Succoth through the years, leaving the comforts of their homes and dwelling in tents or makeshift huts for a period of seven days as a reminder to them of their wanderings. They were never to forget that it was sin and disobedience that had resulted in their forty-year sojourn in the desert. Nor were they to forget how that God had cared for them and provided for their needs during that time.

"You also may be aware of how the Apostle Paul in the New Testament pointed out that your sojourn during your time on earth was also lived in a temporary dwelling, the one known as your earthly body."[64]

We all began to look at each other. Were we hearing this correctly? Could he possibly mean what we thought he meant? We did not have long to wait for the explanation. Aleph had already continued.

"For your seven day observance of the Feast of Tabernacles, you will inhabit your earthly body."

There was an audible gasp from everyone gathered around Aleph. This same communication was being shared with the other groups attending the Feast of Tabernacles for the first time.

"You will feel again the weakness and the limitations that were brought about by the fall. Mind you, you will be protected. You will suffer no injury, no sickness, and you certainly will not die. But you will be reminded of what you have been given, from what state you have been redeemed, and how much you have to be thankful for. The time of your observance begins now."

With that, Aleph disappeared, and with him, all evidence of our supernatural bodies.

At first, I thought I would collapse. John actually did. We all rushed to lift him back to his feet. The difference in the power available in our glorified bodies

---

[64] II Corinthians 5:1-4

to what we were now experiencing was so drastic as to make it difficult to stand. It wasn't that we were feeble by earthly standards, but we had become so accustomed to the virtually unlimited capabilities of our new bodies that this one seemed almost invalid.

Gradually we became acclimated to our new/old selves. There were some groans as we were reintroduced to the likes of arthritis, blurred vision, diminished hearing, muscle aches, joint pain...all those things that had been so common when we were in our earthly bodies, but which we had not experienced now for over seven decades.

Susan was one of the first to speak.

"This was what I heard rumored. I didn't believe it at first, and even when I speculated that it might be true, I didn't fully appreciate the impact. It's been so long since I felt old that I had indeed forgotten what it was like."

John stretched, groaned a little, and said, "Me, too. Being old wasn't any fun before, and it hasn't changed. It's still not fun."

Jessica was frowning. It was the first time I had seen her frown since before the rapture.

"What's wrong?" I asked.

"I don't know," she said. "Something just doesn't feel right. I'm worried."

"Worried about what?" I asked.

"I don't know. It's just a feeling that something's not right."

"I feel it, too," Brad said, "but I don't think it's anything specific. I think that's a part of the old nature. It's been so long since we had any negative feelings, so long since we've had any concerns at all that it feels like something's wrong just because it's not what we are used to."

"I think you may be right, Brad," I said. "The old nature wasn't just about physical limitations. There were the mental and emotional challenges as well – fear, worry, sadness, disappointment, frustration. Those were all done away with in the new body, but now we are subject to them again. It's all a part of remembering what we were delivered from."

Julie had been quiet, taking all this in.

"I'm beginning to understand the purpose of this week. If we forget what we were delivered from, we might begin to take for granted all we have been given. I think what we're saying is that we had already begun that process. This is a reminder of the greatness of our deliverance."

"True," I said. "And as the Jews were reminded that it was their lack of faith and disobedience that caused them to have to wander for forty years in the wilderness, we are reminded that all of the weaknesses, diseases and even death that we endured during our time on earth was also the result of sin and rebellion. We must never forget that. We must be diligent to communicate to those who will grow up in the Kingdom that obedience and faithfulness to God brings His blessing, while disobedience brings a curse."

We all nodded in agreement, and then began the task of making it through the next seven days in our old bodies – which for me meant finding a quiet place to take a nap. I was feeling an exhaustion I had not experienced for fifty years. We had checked into a hotel when we had arrived, so we made our way back to the location. It was only a few blocks, but the older ones – including myself – were out of breath by the time we reached the hotel. I was not the only one needing some rest time.

When I woke up, my first impression was confusion. I was still drowsy, my muscles ached from sleeping awkwardly, and I had the sensation of waking up from a dream. But what was the dream? Had I dreamed about the existence in the new Kingdom? Or was this the dream? It took a few minutes to get my bearings. When I was finally able to look around, everything looked fuzzy. It was then that I realized that I did not have on my glasses. They had materialized when I had reassumed my earthly body, but I had apparently knocked them off while I was sleeping. I found them on the floor beside the bed where I had been sleeping.

I heard conversation in the next room so I went in to see who was here. Jessica was sitting at the dining table along with Brad and Andria. They had come over from their room.

"Good morning," I said. "Is it morning? What time is it?" I realized how long it had been since I had asked that question, how long it had been since time had had any real significance.

Brad laughed. "It's about three in the afternoon, old man. You've been asleep for about four hours."

"Where's everyone else? And watch who you're calling old."

"As far as we know, they're still resting," Jessica said. "They were really wiped out by the time we got back to the hotel. This has been a shock to everyone's system."

Just then, my stomach growled. At first it caught everyone off guard because we didn't Immediately recognize what it was – then everyone burst out laughing.

"Sorry," I said. "It's been a long time since I've been hungry. What do we have to eat?"

"I made a grocery run," said Andria. "We were all famished when we got back to the hotel. There's fruit on the counter, and there's bread and several of the new food items. It's all delicious, of course. At least that hasn't changed."

I made myself a plate of food and joined them at the table. "Do we have a plan?"

"There are morning and evening services at the Tabernacle beginning tomorrow morning," Jessica said.

"Andria and I know the leader of the group that is leading the worship this week," Brad said. "I'm really excited about it. To be able to express our worship for Yeshua with Him actually there – in attendance – in physical form. That's going to be something."

"They say it's an amazing experience," Andria said. "The glory of God fills the entire area. You're engulfed in His presence."

"You know your mom and I experienced something like that when we were in Jerusalem. We were able to sit at Yeshua's feet."

"I know, Dad," said Brad. "You've shared that with us, like a hundred times."

"Oh, so I have." It was very difficult getting used to the limitations of this body, including having some memory lapses.

"I wonder if it will be different experiencing it in an earthly body," Jessica said, half-aloud.

"How can it not be?" I asked. "Everything else is."

****

The remainder of the day was relatively uneventful. We shared our aches and pains and tried to prepare ourselves mentally for the upcoming week. Bedtime came pretty early, particularly with the knowledge that we would rise at six am to prepare for the morning service. We literally had to consciously remind ourselves about things that had once been second nature – baths, brushing our teeth, even eating. With some effort, we all managed to get down to the lobby at the appointed time.

"Are we all ready?" I asked.

"Everyone's here," John said. "Do we have to walk? My rheumatism is acting up this morning."

"No, Dad," Jessica said. "There are transportation shuttles. They're waiting just outside the hotel."

We all helped with Bob and Carolyn, John and Susan. It was strange to see them back in their feeble bodies.

As we settled in for the short commute to the Tabernacle, John said, "You know, it's true. We had all forgotten what we had been redeemed from. The praise to Yeshua is going to come from a different place in our beings, having been reminded of His great provision."

"I believe you're right, John," I said. "And have you thought about the fact that in order to redeem us, He had to assume this form for over thirty years?"

"Oh, wow," Brad said. "I had never even thought about it like that. He took on all our weakness, all our frailty, the ability to suffer pain and weakness and hunger, and endured that – not just for seven days – but for thirty-three years!"

Bob quoted from Philippians concerning Yeshua.

"Who being in the form of God, thought it not robbery to be equal with God: but made Himself of no reputation, and took upon Him the form of a servant, and was made in the likeness of men; and being found in fashion as a man, He humbled Himself, and became obedient unto death, even the death of the cross."[65]

Everyone was misty-eyed by this point. Tears were flowing freely down some cheeks. We rode the rest of the way in silence.

****

The worship time was everything we could have imagined and more. The worship team had written a cantata that traced the ministry of Yeshua from the creation of the universe to the present day, highlighting the creation, the revelation of Himself

---

[65] Philippians 2:5-8

throughout the Old Testament, the preservation of the descendents of Israel, the incarnation, His sinless life, His offering of Himself as the sacrificial Lamb on Calvary, His triumphant resurrection and the establishment of the earthly Kingdom. It was indescribably magnificent!

We had experienced times of worship during our earthly sojourn, but nothing of this magnitude! Of course, the main difference was the presence of Yeshua Himself. It wasn't just that His glory was visibly present – although I must say that was awesome! It was that His presence gave focus to our worship. So often on earth, we had been distracted by the "performance" of the singers, or by thoughts of what others around us were doing or thinking. Not here. Everyone was supremely aware that this was all about Yeshua. It was all about our expressing our worship and praise and thanksgiving to Him. Having been reminded of the great sacrifice that He had made in order for us to be here, our praise took on an even higher expression.

By the time the service ended, we were all physically drained, but spiritually exhilarated! This was indeed going to be a wonderful week!

CHAPTER 7

The first hundred years of the Kingdom Age were years of tremendous innovation. After the initial clean-up and construction, efforts had turned toward invention and creativity. We had rapidly reimplemented the technology of the 21st century, and innovation had increased exponentially as we moved through the first century KA.

Some of the more notable advances had been in transportation and communication. As had been predicted, everything was now solar powered, so there was never any need for electricity, gas or other fuels. Hovercrafts and jetpacks were the modes of transportation used by most individuals and families, while space shuttles were available for everything from around the world travel to vacations to the newly constructed space stations. Most communication was done via astral projection, which enabled you to have a virtual face-to-face conversation with anyone from anywhere on the globe.

Everything was manufactured to the highest degree of excellence, so there were virtually no repairs ever needed. While there was no such thing as "planned obsolescence", the innovations at one point were coming so rapidly that it was difficult for individuals to stay up to date with the latest and greatest. As time went by, things slipped into a more sustainable pace.

Attentions turned to enjoyment of the environment with which we had been blessed, and the raising of families.

We had been on the verge of an information explosion before the rapture occurred, but now that all efforts were coordinated and orchestrated for the good of humanity, the progress had been extraordinary. We often talked about how much time, energy, resources and efforts had been wasted on earth pursuing means of warfare and violence, not to mention the tremendous investments in seeking cures for diseases. All of these efforts were now being channeled into positive areas.

Our regular family outing was the opportunity for everyone to be updated on what was going on. We had decided to meet at one of the parks that had been constructed in the rebuilt city of Buenos Aires. The city had, of course, been the capital city of Argentina prior to the Rapture, and now served as the base of operations for Yeshua's governing body in this area. Much of the reconstruction was done in keeping with the architectural style of the previous era. Needless to say, it was very impressive.

It was a beautiful park, filled with trees and flowers, species from all over the world, since climate was no longer limiting factor. In addition, there were new species that had been developed and cultivated by the agriculture teams. Bob and Carolyn would be able to point out some of the attributes of the new species, having been involved with the teams that developed some of them.

As we arrived, there was the usual hugging and greeting. We had our family outings once a month, but not everyone was at each one. Sometimes individuals or couples were travelling or involved in other activities, so I was pleased to see that everyone had made it this time.

"Ross, Jessica, so good to see you again," Bob said. "And here are my beautiful grandchildren! I'm sure you've all grown at least a millimeter!"

He referred to them all as his grandchildren, although technically Hart and Grace were great-grandchildren. This had become common practice among all of the families because of the multi-generational connections. It was just too tedious to say "great-great-great-great grandchildren".

His reference to them having grown a millimeter had become sort of a family joke. Because of the slowing of the aging process and the frequency that we all got together, it was virtually impossible to tell any difference in the children from one visit to the next. But as they say, old habits die hard, and the grandparents had almost always commented on how the children had grown between their earthly visits.

Not to say there had not been some change over the years. A hundred years into the Kingdom Age, the children had aged ten earth years. Hart and Grace were now the equivalent of fourteen in earth years, and Lizzie was ten. And they were handfuls! Bundles of energy and curiosity – and still with enough of the traits of self-will to make them challenging at times.

The children were always the center of attention whenever we got together, especially at the beginning. Later, they would wander off to play or explore and leave the adults to our own conversations. Hart and Grace had entered into those years of transition – not a child any longer, but not quite an adult. We all remembered the challenges of that stage of life for ourselves on earth. Here, it lasted for fifty to sixty years! Lizzie was still in little girl mode – bright, precocious, and absolutely adorable.

"Come give your Grandma a hug," Susan called to the children.

Lizzie and Grace ran into her arms, squealing with delight. Hart was a little more reserved. He was beginning to think of himself as a young man, and wasn't quite as eager for the public displays of affection.

Susan had come to recognize this on previous visits. "And how's my young man?" she said to Hart, extending her hand. He beamed and shook it warmly.

"I'm just fine, Grandma. It's really good to see you."

"Let's break out the food," Brad said. "I hear we've got some new tastes to try."

Everybody laughed. Brad would always be Brad!

As we spread the lunch table, the grandparents took the opportunity to catch up on what had been going on in the lives of the children.

"Hart, are you enjoying soccer?" Carolyn asked.

His face lit up. "Oh, yes m'am! We're almost halfway into the season and we're in second place. That's out of twenty teams in our division, you know. So that's pretty good, isn't it?"

"Well, more than pretty good, I'd say. I think that's outstanding."

"The leagues are very competitive because everyone's physical bodies are so perfect. Almost every game is close and is often just decided by whoever happens to be leading when time runs out. I scored the winning goal in our last game with only eight seconds left in the game!"

"That's my boy!" said John, and then in a little more subdued tone after getting a little sideways glance from Susan, "Of course, the important thing is just to always do your best and enjoy the competition and the camaraderie."

"Right, Grandpa. That's what Dad always says."

"Well, your Dad is right," Susan said. "You make sure you always listen to him. And what about you, Grace? What are you involved in now?"

"We're studying microbiology and thermodynamics in school right now, but what I really enjoy is ice skating."

She rolled off the microbiology and thermodynamics as if it were no big deal. And in a sense, it wasn't. With multiple years available for their education, with minds clear of the destructive elements of the fall, and with no time wasted on unruly students or politically correct social engineering, the educational system was a thousand times more effective than it had been previously. So the real reaction from everyone was about the ice-skating.

"Ice skating?" Susan said. "Now there's something new."

"Yes, m'am. We go twice a week. There's a frozen lake in Juneau where a lot of the kids like to go."

"Juneau? Juneau, Alaska?"

"Yes, m'am. I think that's the only one there is. Mom & Dad take us sometimes, and sometimes Julie takes us. Hart and Lizzie go, too. Hart's thinking about ice hockey for next season, but Lizzie and I just like to skate. Sometimes they have skaters there who skated in the Olympics. They show us how to do tricks and stuff."

Lizzie chimed in. "I'm going to be an Olympic skater when I grow up. I'm going to do jumps, and spins and pillowettes." With each word, she added her own visible portrayal of each move.

"You mean 'pirouettes', honey," Jessica corrected.

"That's what I said," and with that, finished with a flourish of three more 'pillowettes'.

"Time to eat!" Julie announced.

We all gathered around the table and each took turns giving thanks. My favorite time was always when it came to Lizzie.

"Thank you, Lord Jesus, for everything. Thank you for the food. Thank you for my family. Thank you for loving me and giving me so many things to say 'thank you' for. Amen."

"Amen. Let's eat!" You would think Brad had been starved as a child.

After we finished eating, the kids asked to be excused from the table to go play. They joined a group of children down near a pond where some were swimming and others engaged in a game that I did not recognize using a Frisbee shaped disc and a long pole. There were also several animals that the children were playing with. In addition to the usual array of dogs and cats, there was also a zebra, a couple of giraffes and a hippopotamus – and that's just the ones I could see.

Jessica gazed out at the scene and said, "How wonderful to be able to release the children to play without any fear or worry about injury or foul play."

"Indeed, it is," I responded. "It is just another of the many benefits of our environment."

We all talked for quite a while about what was going on in the different areas of ministry. Even if it had not been extended times since we had seen each other, the innovations were coming so rapidly that there was always something new to report. At times, we would stop and just enjoy the music that wafted over the landscape. The praise and worship teams were everywhere, and if you focused, you could always hear their melodic sounds. It was as if everyone had a radio tuner inside their heads, and it was only necessary to "tune in" in order to hear the music.

Brad, Andria and Julie's team had been selected to present the worship at the next Feast of Tabernacles, and they were beside themselves with excitement.

"It's going to be amazing," Andria said. "I hope you'll all be able to be there."

"Are you kidding?" I said. "Of course we'll be there – and right up front!"

John had been watching the children play and not really paying attention to what we had been discussing. When he rejoined the conversation, it was obvious his thoughts had been elsewhere.

"What about their spiritual progress?" The question was somewhat generally directed at me, Jessica, Brad and Andria.

"What do you mean? Whose?" Andria asked.

"Why, the children, of course. What is their spiritual progress? Have they all surrendered their hearts to Christ?"

Jessica spoke up first. "Dad, we know you're concerned…"

"Of course I'm concerned! I was saved at eight years of age, and here my grandchildren are, ten and fourteen…yes, I'm concerned. Shouldn't I be?"

I intervened at this point. "John, you do understand that time has a whole new perspective here in the Kingdom. Not only do things move a lot more slowly, but also there is not that element of uncertainty concerning the future. On earth there was an urgency because we were not promised another day. We never knew which day would be our last, which opportunity would be our last. Here, things are different. We are assured that our children will live and mature and reach that point where they will be able to make their own choice. Having said that, speaking for Lizzie, she is very spiritually inclined. Her heart is tender; she already has a true and deep love for Jesus. I am not worried about her decision when she is ready to make it."

John turned toward Brad and Andria. "And what about Hart and Grace?"

"Gramps, Hart and Grace are going to be fine," Brad said. "Grace has always had a receptive heart and spirit. If we pushed her, I'm sure she would respond positively right now, but we want that to come from her."

"Fine," John said, "and what about Hart?"

There was a hesitation that caught me off guard. Brad exchanged glances with Andria before he continued.

"Hart is going to be fine. He's going through a phase right now. Several of his friends are Mortals who were born to Adamites and this is the only existence they have ever known. While that certainly has its advantages, it also means that they have no experience with any other reality other than this one.

"He's developed a close friendship with one boy in particular – Jason. Jason's parents are actually tribulation Saints. They were martyred for refusing to take the mark of the Antichrist. Their entry into the Kingdom was both dramatic and traumatic. It took them quite a while after the start of the Kingdom Age to learn and get acclimated to the truths that we were all raised on. Their ability to explain the virtues of living the

Christian life is quite limited. The only Christian existence they have known prior to the Kingdom was the most violent, wicked era of all of history."

Andria spoke up with her own perception of the situation.

"The boys are young," she said, "and they don't really understand the concepts of right and wrong. They're just like we were when we were teenagers – they want to find out things for themselves. They want to push the boundaries. They want to live their own lives and make their own choices. We talk to them as often as we can without badgering them, as do Jason's own parents. Ultimately, they will each make their own decisions. We are confident that with the influences and prayers that Hart is receiving from this family, he will give his life to Christ in due time."

We all sat there in solemn silence. We all knew the truth of what Andria had just said, but hearing it said aloud brought it home in a stunning way. Over the next few centuries, Hart – and multiplied millions like him – would be confronted with the choice that had been presented to each of us during our lifetime: what would they do with Jesus Christ? Would they acknowledge Him for who He is? Would they willingly submit and surrender to Him as Lord? Or would they rebel and choose their own path?

"Let's pray," Jessica whispered.

We bowed in the grass, and solemnly entered the presence of Yeshua, interceding for our children and grandchildren, and for Jason, and for the multitudes that they represented.

CHAPTER 8

The family's attention turned toward the upcoming Feast of Tabernacles. Having already attended on more than one occasion, we were prepared for our week of "dwelling in tents." It had become a time of reflection when we as a family would spend much of the week meditating and reflecting on Yeshua's great redemption.

This year two things would make the week different from the others. We were all excited about Brad, Andria and Julie's praise team leading in worship. And we had also discussed the possibility of using this time when we were back in mortal form to probe whether or not there were elements of that existence that would help us to better communicate with the Mortals of the Kingdom Age, including our own children and grandchildren. In addition, this was the first time the children had accompanied us, and it would be their first exposure to us outside our glorified bodies.

We all met in the hotel room for our first meal after our arrival – and our reentry into our mortal bodies. The young folks were in mild shock the first time they saw us. We had tried to prepare them ahead of time, but they really had no frame of reference to understand what we were trying to communicate. Hart and Grace had vague memories of life prior to the Rapture, but for Lizzie, this was her first exposure to what life had been like.

"Dad, is that really you?" Lizzie asked.

"Yes, honey, it's me – your old Dad."

"And Grandpa...and Grandma...you're so...so..."

"Old, honey," said Bob, "the word you're looking for is 'old'."

"And not just old," Carolyn said, "but frail, and with a lot of weaknesses and limitations."

Hart and Grace were still trying to pull up deep seated and long ago forgotten memories of times gone by.

"These were the bodies we lived in prior to the Rapture," I said. "They lasted for seventy, eighty, maybe even as long as a hundred years. But the older they got the more frail they became, the more susceptible they were to injury and disease – but you don't even know what disease is, do you? At any rate, bottom line is – they wore out. And when they did, they died. Had your mother and I not lived in the generation that saw the Rapture take place, that's what would have happened to us."

"Your grandmother and I did die," John said, "along with all of our ancestors and the generations before us. The souls of the Saints were protected in the presence of Yeshua until the day of the Rapture, when we were resurrected in our glorified bodies."

"And so why are you back in those bodies now?" Hart asked. "What's the purpose of this?"

"It's a reminder," Jessica said, "a reminder of what we were, and what we've been given. You see, son, the condition we were in before with its weakness and disease and death were all the result of disobedience to the laws of God. None of us ever wants to forget that. We do not want to forget that it is only by the grace and forgiveness purchased by the sacrifice of Yeshua that we are here today."

I said, "And now let's eat and get some rest – another new concept I'll try to explain to you – and prepare for tomorrow's worship."

****

The morning's worship was beyond all imagination. As always, and as it should be, the focal point was the presence of Yeshua and the manifestation of His glory. But as the Scripture spoke of Him inhabiting the praise of His people, there was a reciprocating relationship between His glory and the praise offered to Him. As the praise team and the assembled worshippers sounded waves of praise, His glory would radiate even more, soliciting even louder and more enthusiastic praise, which would then generate even greater revelation of His majesty.

The praise team had incorporated all the languages of the earth in their songs, symbolizing the universality of His Lordship, and the worldwide scope of His Kingdom.   The children were actually able to understand more of the lyrics than we were. Not being in our glorified bodies, we no longer had the ability to understand anything beyond the abilities we had on earth.   The children, on the other hand, had learned several languages during the course of their schooling.

We arrived back at the hotel physically spent, but on a spiritual high.

"That was intense!" John said. "You kids did an amazing job. I believe that was the most connected I have ever been in any worship time."

"Thanks, Grandpa," Julie said. "It's just such an honor to be able to lead in worship in the very presence of Yeshua."

Brad started humming a praise chorus from back during our time on earth, and before long, we were all singing along.

"In the presence of Jehovah,
God Almighty, Prince of Peace;
Troubles vanish, hearts are mended,
in the presence of the King."

****

One of the highlights of the time spent in Israel was getting to interact with the heroes we had read about in the Old and New Testament. We were all out walking one afternoon, enjoying the ambiance of the place where Yeshua had walked when He was here the first time, when we saw a large crowd gathering near the eastern gate of the city.

"I wonder what's going on over there," Julie said.

"Let's go see," Hart said, and dashed off ahead. The youngsters all took off after him.

"Well," Bob said, "I guess we're going to see." With that, we older folks started making our way toward the crowd, although at a much more modest pace.

As we got to the outer edge of the crowd, Jessica asked someone, "What's going on? Who is the center of attention?"

Not being in our glorified bodies, we had lost the ability to instantly recognize individuals and interpret situations.

The answer came back, "It's Methuselah."

Methuselah![66] The oldest man who had ever lived on earth! Nine hundred and sixty-nine years! The eighth generation from the first man, Adam. The grandfather of

---

[66] Genesis 5:21-27

Noah. No wonder he was drawing such a crowd. He had already begun talking.

"As you've been told, my time on earth was in a much different environment than the one you live in, even different to the one that some of you experienced during your life here in the pre-Kingdom age . Prior to the great flood, the earth was a totally different place. The aging process was similar to what you are experiencing now...much slower."

He laughed as he said, "I didn't even have my first son until I was a hundred and eighty-six years old!"

There were some chuckles and a few gasps from the crowd.

"What was it like, living such a long life?" came a question from one of the Mortals near the front of the crowd.

"It was a blessing...and a curse. Because Adam lived to be nine hundred and thirty years old, I was alive for the last two hundred and fifty years of his life. I had the opportunity to hear from his very lips the story of the Garden of Eden and the early days of creation. I was blessed to see not only my children and grandchildren, but also my great- grandchildren. You will get to experience the same thing, along with the blessing of seeing and getting to know many of the generations that preceded you. But the curse was in watching the deterioration of my society."

His eyes took on a deep sadness as he seemed to be speaking to no one in particular – maybe just to himself.

"Our world was much different from this one in more ways than one. Yahweh had revealed His plan and His will, but there were so few that were interested in following Him. I watched as an entire society, including virtually all of my own family and descendents, my friends, everyone I knew except for faithful Noah...they all turned from the ways of Yahweh to wicked rebellion. Demonic forces contributed to the corruption of the very nature of human genetics[67].

"By the time I neared the end of my life, the world had totally abandoned any pretext of righteousness. They tried to outdo one another in their expression of their evil life styles.[68] The last few years of my life were ones of sorrow and despair.

"I had lived too long. I had lived to see things that I had never wanted to see. And I knew the judgment of Yahweh was coming. It wasn't difficult to imagine. If I had been Yahweh, I would have destroyed them a lot sooner. However, in His mercy He gave a final warning

---

[67] Genesis 6:2
[68] Genesis 6:5

through my grandson, Noah. For one hundred and twenty years, he worked on that ark – hammering and prophesying, hammering and prophesying. I watched him put that final peg in the last board on the ark, even saw the animals beginning to gather."

"And then what happened?" The question jarred him back into the moment.

"And then what happened?? And then I died! And then the great flood came! And everyone I had ever known, all my family, all my friends, everyone except Noah and his family were destroyed."

"That's awful! What a tragic story! We've been told of Yahweh's great mercy. That doesn't sound very merciful."

These words had come from another Mortal. They often had difficulty relating to the concepts of sin and judgment.

"Be careful with your judgments!" Methuselah scolded. "The flood was indeed evidence of a merciful Creator. Had Yahweh not destroyed them when He did, had He allowed the course of the world to continue as it was going, when Noah died, there would have been no one righteous left on the earth. There would have been no one to receive the message of Yahweh's grace and His plan for the redemption of humanity. The entire human race would have been lost. Because He brought judgment when He did, you are here today. Beware the mind that questions the righteous dealings of Him who is Supreme Wisdom."

That brought an end to the questions, and to Methuselah's discourse.   He excused himself and retreated into the Temple.

As we walked away, the young people were whispering among themselves.

"Wow, that was pretty intense," Grace said.

"Really!" Hart exclaimed. "All that stuff about sin and judgment and destruction. It seems to me there must have been another way to handle that situation. I mean, did the whole world really have to be destroyed?"

"You really shouldn't question Yahweh, Hart," Grace responded. "You heard what Methuselah said. If Yahweh had not acted when He did, the entire human race would have been lost."

"I heard what he said. I'm just not sure I'm convinced. I mean, what's he supposed to say? He's a part of that generation that rebelled. And it was such a long time ago. I'm not sure it has any relevance to us today. There's not any sin or rebellion going on here."

"No, I guess not," Grace said. Then to herself, "At least not any that anyone can see."

CHAPTER 9

Mid-second century K.A. (Kingdom Age) is when the shadows of the upcoming challenges began to creep into the brightness of our glorious day. The children born in the Kingdom – the Mortals – were now entering their teen years. Majorities of them were very receptive to the message of Christ's redemption and submitted their lives to Him at an early age, or at least were well on the way to doing so. But there were some – a small number at this point – who were more resistant.

Having all been raised by Christian parents, surrounded by Godly influences, and without the temptations of worldly philosophies or the direct influence of Satan, they were certainly not the problem that much of their last generation on earth had been. There were no outward displays of rebellion. There was certainly no drug culture. There was no sexual revolution.

Yet, there were signs. Because they had not embraced the rule of Christ in their own hearts, you could sometimes sense resistance to the law as expressed from the throne room in Jerusalem. Because there was no personal connection to Yeshua through their own relationship with Him, and little recognition of the fact that the blessed existence they were experiencing was the result of His sacrifice, their reaction to the praise and worship of Yeshua often did not come from their heart, but from ritual and expectation.

In many ways, they reminded me of the Church in the closing days prior to the Rapture.[69] For many of the professing Christians of the last days, church had become "some place you go" rather than "something you are." It had become all about the entertainment, the emotion, the competition among local churches to see who could draw the biggest crowds, who could build the biggest building, who could put on the most elaborate production. For others it had been all about the social gospel – feeding the hungry, helping the needy, saving the planet.   Well over half of the professing church at the time of the Rapture were not even truly saved, and thus were left behind to meet their fate at the hands of the Antichrist.

This developing aspect of our society became the focus of our conversation when we gathered for our family get-together in 150 K.A., this time in a mountain chalet in the Swiss Alps. Hart and Grace, now the equivalent of nineteen, and Lizzie, now fifteen, had invited several of their friends, including Jason, to join us on our retreat. They were all off skating and skiing and had left the rest of us to our discussion.

"It's hard for me to understand," John was saying, "how anyone can look around them at the perfection of

---

[69] II Timothy 3:1-5

the environment we live in and want to change anything. And I'm not just talking about climate. I'm talking about true righteousness, perfect justice, peace and tranquility – what's the problem with any of that?"

"I don't think anyone would say there is a problem with any of those things," Brad responded. "But you have to remember that until the human nature is submitted to Christ there is a self-centeredness there. Not necessarily self-centered in the form of being selfish or egotistic – although it can certainly manifest itself that way – but just a desire for self expression. It's a desire to choose for themselves what path they will walk, and express themselves in the way that they would choose. Until that part of a person is willingly submitted to the authority of Christ, any attempt to restrict who they are or what they can do is going to be resisted."

We had heard and discussed these same concepts before, often with our own children and grandchildren.

"We see that, son," I said. "And for that matter, we saw it in our own earthly experience. After we were saved, we would often look around at the unsaved and wonder how anyone could or would refuse the gracious offer of salvation and eternal life. But much of the reason for that is that they did not want to give up control. They wanted to make their own choices and decisions without the restrictions that they saw associated with the Bible, God's 'rulebook'. They were not able to see without the enlightenment of the Holy Spirit that what they saw as restrictions were actually protections – that God only forbade things that would ultimately cause harm."

"And even if they did recognize that at some level, many were simply not willing to surrender that control," Julie added.

As if her words were not enough, the pensiveness in her eyes reflected her personal sadness as to that reality.

Bob and Carol had been quiet up to this point, but now Bob spoke up.

"There's at least one other factor that we haven't discussed. Part of our perspective comes from the fact that we've seen the other side. We've experienced firsthand the effects of sinful choices. We've seen the calamity of war and the destruction of crime and the rampage of disease. We know about divorce and child abuse and political corruption. We've witnessed the tragedies of alcoholism and drug addiction. These kids don't know anything about that.

"They've grown up in what we know to be a perfect environment, exempt from all of those things, but in their minds it's, 'What if there's something better?' It's the old 'grass is always greener' syndrome. Only for them, they can't actually see over the fence – it's all just fantasy."

John spoke back up. "So again we are back to the central question for us as a family: how do we ensure that our children and grandchildren aren't swallowed up by the deception?"

"Lizzie is sound," Jessica said. "She is growing in Christian graces every day and shows no desire whatsoever to even associate with anyone who is not fully committed to Christ. I cannot even imagine that she will not surrender her heart to Christ in the very near future."

"Well," Andria said, "as for Grace, she is showing every sign of a committed Christian. I truly believe that the only reason she has not yet fully surrendered is that she is waiting on Hart. She and he have always been more than just brother and sister. Certainly some of it is biological, being twins. I believe some of their connection has to do with being transported to this new environment at such an early age and spending so much time growing up together. I believe that somewhere in her mind, either consciously or subconsciously, she is thinking that they will make that commitment together."

"And so that brings us back to Hart," John said.

"Yes, it does," Brad sighed, "as it always seems to."

"I see he's still hanging out with Jason," Susan said. "Do you think that's a good idea?"

"I don't know if it's a good idea," Brad said. "Our hope was, and continues to be, that Hart and Grace would be a positive influence on Jason. Andria and I take every opportunity to try to influence him. His parents have matured greatly in their own faith, so he is getting some good influence there as well.

"And it's not that he's a bad boy. He is never openly disrespectful of any element of our faith. He seems very intelligent and open – even receptive – to the discussion about the righteous aspect of the reign of Christ. He just still has a lot of questions."

About that time, the kids got back from their outing. Laughing and joking, they streamed into the chalet, obviously unaware of the seriousness of the conversation we had just been involved in.

"Well, hi, everyone," Carolyn said. "How were the slopes and the lake?"

"Awesome!" "Unbelievable!" "Perfect!" They were all speaking at once.

"Thank you so much for inviting us to come with you," Jason said.

"Oh, yeah," several of the others echoed. "This has been great! Thanks a lot."

"You're welcome," I answered. "Glad you all could come."

Jessica said, "Why don't you all go and change out of your gear and I'll make hot chocolate for everyone?"

"Sure. Sounds great."

They all took off, the boys to one side of the chalet and the girls to the other. Jessica almost dropped the pot of water as she overheard Lizzie whispering to Grace as they walked by.

"Don't you think that Jason is just the cutest? And so smart!"

CHAPTER 10

The remainder of our time at the chalet was enjoyable, mixed with occasional bits of strained communication. We did not delve further into the specifics of the children's lives, or the complexity of the overall situation as it related to their generation. We did, however, look for any opportunities there might be to engage them in conversations of a spiritual nature. One such opportunity presented itself as we gathered for breakfast on the morning of our last day at the chalet.

"Wow! Look at this spread!" Jason said, as the teenagers entered the breakfast area. "You Waters really know how to set a table!"

"Why, thank you, Jason," Jessica said. "Several of us had a hand in this one."

About that time John, Bob, Brad and I came in from the outside deck.

"That is some view," Bob said. "I think this may be my favorite spot of all the ones we've been to so far."

"Ranks right up there for me, too," John said. "I've always loved the mountains."

"Well, if we young folks get a vote, this place gets an 'aye' from me," Grace said. "This whole time has been wonderful."

All the young people chimed in with their voices of agreement about the outing, expressing their thanks again, hoping we all could do it again, etc.

"Of course we can," I said. "We still have over 800 years of time to enjoy the great provisions of the Lord. Now what say we have breakfast? I thought since it was our last day together on this trip, it might be nice if we all took a turn giving thanks to Yeshua for His blessings, for giving us the privilege to share this time together."

Everyone bowed their heads, and beginning with the elder members of the family, the prayer chain proceeded around the table. When it got to the teenagers, a couple of them stumbled a little as they got out a few words of thanks. It was fairly obvious they were not totally comfortable praying in front of others, but they got through it. When it came to Jason, there was a bit of awkward silence. Then he looked up, caught my eye, and said, "Mr. Waters, sir, if it's ok, could you pass over me? I'm not real good at this."

"Sure, son. It's no problem. Lizzie?"

"I think I'll pass too, Dad, if that's ok."

I don't know if anyone saw my eyes mist over or not. I had always loved hearing Lizzie pray. But I swallowed and managed to get out, "Of course, honey. No one ever has to pray. Amen, everyone?"

"Amen."

It was a little more subdued than normal, but as we got into breakfast, the tension eased and things got closer to normal. The teens were cutting up and the adults' conversation turned to plans upon our return.

We were nearing the end of breakfast, during a lull in the conversation when Jason got my attention.

"What can I do for you, Jason? Do you need me to pass you something?"

"Oh, no sir. I've had plenty. You said something earlier that I wanted to ask you about if you don't mind."

"Not at all. What is it?"

"You said something about having 800 years left to enjoy our surroundings. First of all, how do you know that? And why do we only have 800 years?"

"Good question. Although I'm a little surprised you haven't already been given the answers to these questions."

"Well, sir, I have, in a way. My parents have tried to explain it to me, and of course, it's discussed in school, but I still don't really understand it, and I thought you might be able to explain it better. Hart tells me you were a preacher or something before, you know – back in the old world."

"That's right, I was. And you have a lot of other experience here at this table as well. So I, for one, would love to try to answer any questions you have. How about the rest of you guys? Anybody else got question?"

"Oh, yes sir," several of them responded.

"OK, what do you say we all help clear the table then meet out on the patio for some discussion?"

"Sounds good." "Great!" "Let's do it!" The enthusiasm was encouraging.

As we were clearing the table, the Saints all connected telepathically for corporate prayer. This could be a pivotal time in these young lives. After everything was put away, we all gathered out on the patio.

"OK," I said. "First of all let me be clear that this is not a lecture. Questions and discussion are welcomed, and I'm encouraging my fellow Saints to chime in whenever they feel like it.

"Let's start with the question on the table. How do I know how much time we have left in the Kingdom Age? There are really two ways to answer that question. The simplest way is to tell you that Yeshua, when the Kingdom Age first began, told us that it would last for one thousand years."

"And you were there to hear that personally?" one of the teenagers asked.

"Yes, I was, as were all of the Saints. Everyone here with the exception of you teenagers were here when the Kingdom Age began, and heard the Lord declare that we had one thousand years to enjoy the pleasures of the kingdom."

"You said there were two ways," Jason said. "What is the other?"

"The other way goes back into, what is for you all, the dark past, the time before the Kingdom Age began. We Saints all lived for different periods of time in the old world. At that time, our only connection with Yahweh was through His revealed Word, the Bible. Along with many instructions and communications concerning Yayweh's dealings with mankind, there were also prophetic Scriptures dealing with what would happen in the future – including some details about the age in which we live now, the Kingdom Age."

"Yes, indeed," Bob said. "Back in the day one of my favorite pastimes was studying the Bible to see what it had to say about the future. The words that we were reading in my day had been written anywhere from two thousand to over five thousand years before we read them. Yet we were able to watch them unfold before our very eyes."

"Right," I said. "And part of those prophetic Scriptures told about this time was that it would last for one thousand years.[70] So when Yeshua said that to us at the beginning of the Age, it was no surprise at all. It was just confirmation of what we had already been told in the Bible. The rest is just math. We're in year 150 K.A. We have 850 years left."

There were a few moments of silence as this information was digested and compared mentally with what had been shared with them previously.

"Then what?" It was Jason again. He had apparently become the spokesman for the group. "What happens in 850 years?"

"Can I start this one?" John asked.

"Of course you can," I said.

"OK, kids, this is the most important part of the story. There's a being that you have heard about, but you've never actually seen or been exposed to. He goes by many names – Lucifer, Satan, Devil – but what you really need to know about him is that he is the opposite of Yeshua. He is the embodiment of evil and wickedness and sin."

"What is sin?" This was Jason again.

"Sin is anything that is contrary to the word of Yeshua. I know it's hard for you young people to comprehend, because you've never really been exposed to sin. But in the old world, most of the people who lived were not followers of Yeshua. They lived their

---

[70] Revelation 20:5-7

lives either in ignorance of His word, or in disobedience to His word."

There was a little bit of uncomfortable foot shuffling and floor staring at this point. Most of these young people had never been involved in any discussion where disobedience to Yeshua was even mentioned. The very thought was a frightening one.

John continued. "Lucifer is the ultimate law breaker. As I said, he is the opposite of Yeshua. So if the Lord says, 'Right', Lucifer says, 'Wrong.' If the Lord says, 'Up', he says 'Down'. If the Lord says, 'Do this,' Lucifer says, 'Don't do this.' And anytime you choose Lucifer's way, it's sin. Understand?"

"Sort of. But you said we've never had any contact with Lucifer. So what's any of that got to do with the question?"

"Two things. First of all, while Lucifer is the prime example of sinful actions, he is not the only one who can sin in these ways. Any of you who would choose your own way instead of Yeshua's is doing the same thing as Lucifer. But the second part of the answer will finally address your question concerning what happens in 850 years. The reason why you have never had any encounter with Lucifer is that he was bound and restrained when the Kingdom Age began.[71] His influence was never to be felt during this time. But he

---

[71] Revelation 20:1-2

was not destroyed. Toward the end of the Age, he will be released and will once more have access to the world we live in."[72]

"But why? That makes no sense. If he is so evil and wicked, why would Yeshua ever allow him to come back?"

I was glad Julie stepped in here. A softer tone might take some of the edge off what was becoming a very intense discussion.

"Jason, the will of Yeshua has always been that those who serve Him would do so willingly, out of a heart of love. All of us," gesturing to all the Saints, "made that choice back in the old world. Without ever having physically seen Yeshua or Yahweh, we were drawn to Him through what was revealed of Him in the Bible, and what was communicated to us through His Spirit. Those of you who were born, or who grew up from a young age here in the Kingdom, will each have the opportunity to make that same choice. We hope all of you do so. But for the ones who do not, for those who fail to commit to follow Yeshua, they will be given an opportunity at the close of the Kingdom to choose to follow Lucifer."

"And then what?"

I stepped back in here. "Then, Jason, there is going to be one final battle. All of those who choose to side with Lucifer in that battle will be destroyed.[73] Those

---

[72] Revelation 20:3, 7-8

of us who are on the side of Yeshua will enter into the next phase of the plan of Yahweh – eternity."

Another period of silence.

Jason looked around at the group of teenagers. "Did you know all of this?"

All of our children had heard it many times. Some of the others had heard bits and pieces, some more than others.

"That's a lot to process," Jason said. "I think I'm going to have some more questions. Can we do this again?"

"Absolutely," I said. "As a matter of fact, why don't we make it a regular thing? How would you all like to get together once a week for a while?"

"I'd like that," Jason said. "Yes, sir. I'd like that a lot."

---

[73] Revelation 20:9

CHAPTER 11

The next few weeks proved to be very interesting. Apparently, there were many of the Mortals who had questions about the past and how that related to their present and future. What started as an intimate gathering of our children and a few of their friends soon grew to a crowd of over a thousand. We moved our group to an outdoor arena that was more accommodating. We soon became aware that there were similar groups springing up all around the world. The young people really wanted to hear about our experiences on pre-Kingdom earth and how those experiences related to the remainder of the Kingdom Age and beyond.

Often these discussions ventured into areas other than theological discussions about righteousness and the government of Yeshua. Sometimes the discussions would involve the different forms of governments – monarchies, dictatorships, democracies, autocracies, etc. That would inevitably lead to a discussion of the various philosophies of economics – capitalism, communism, socialism.

"So if I understand this correctly," one of the Mortals commented, "what we are actually living in is a dictatorship with a form of socialist economy. It's certainly not a democracy or even a republic, because we have little or no say in the laws that govern us."

This was not the first time I had heard this type of analogy, but it was disconcerting nonetheless. I waited for the buzz of interaction among the group to quiet before I answered.

"The mistake you are making is trying to fit our current situation into the mold of examples that you are looking at from our previous existence. The options that we had to choose from in our day had to consider that humans were in the positions of power. All of those humans, regardless of their degree of morality or even their relationship to Yeshua, were flawed. All of the governments, all of the economic models had to deal with humanity in a fallen state.

"In one sense, the most efficient form of government has always been some form of autocracy where the decisions were being made by one person or a very small group of people. The inherent problem with this is expressed in a saying that we had in those days, 'Power corrupts. And absolute power corrupts absolutely.' Because humans were fallible and easily corrupted, the best way to protect the masses was to ensure that power was distributed over a broad base so that there was some element of restraint on the amount of power that anyone could possess. This was the principle behind the separation of powers that we tried to achieve in the government of the United States. Unfortunately, even that proved ultimately ineffective in preventing corruption and abuse of power."

"But you still haven't really addressed my question," he responded. "Aren't we living under a dictatorship?"

"Actually the correct definition of our government is a theocracy. It is the rule of God Himself expressed in the physical manifestation of Yeshua. The difference is that we are not dealing with a fallen man. Yeshua is perfect righteousness, perfect justice without any taint of sin. It is impossible for Him to be corrupted, impossible for Him to act in any way other than what is right and just, and therefore impossible for His laws to be anything other than what is in the absolute best interest for all mankind."

One of the other Mortals spoke up. "But you do have to admit that is a type of dictatorship. We don't have any input into any of the laws that govern us."

"And what if you did?" I asked. "What would you change? How would you make things better than they are right now?"

He hesitated for several seconds as the attention of the group turned toward him. "Well, I'm not saying I would change anything. I'm just making the observation that we don't have a voice."

"I am intrigued by the benefits of capitalism, however." This was Jason. "It seems to me that it is the most effective means of maximizing productivity. Give people a reason to produce. Our system that we are operating under does not reward effort. We could be producing much more product, and many more innovations, if everyone were more motivated."

"But to what end?" I said. "We lack for nothing. There is no pressure on anyone to sacrifice family time or relationships. Believe me; I still remember enough to know that those things do not bring increased satisfaction. As for innovation, we can barely keep up with the pace of innovation now. Inventions and improvements on existing products are being produced so rapidly that the populace cannot even absorb them. What would be gained by implementing a system targeted with increasing productivity?"

"That's true enough, I guess, but I'm bothered sometimes when I see some people working much harder than others while everyone has access to the same level of consumption. Somehow it just doesn't seem fair."

"Your concept of fairness doesn't allow for the fact that we live in Yeshua's grace. No matter how much a person might work or contribute, they would never be worthy of the blessings we've been given. So rather than fairness on a relative scale that matches contribution to benefit, we live in a state of grace that says regardless of contribution, everything we receive is a gift.[74]   That frees people to contribute at whatever level they desire, and still experience the full benefit of Yeshua's blessing.   And as I said, it's working very well. Productivity is far outstripping demand."

"You're right, of course.   But it does make for interesting conversation, don't you think?"

"Possibly.   But remember – sometimes there's a fine line between interesting and dangerous."

[74] Matthew 20:1-16

CHAPTER 12

"Let's get away for a while." Jessica had not said anything like this in some time. "We've been so involved in the lives of the children and grandchildren for the last few months. How about just some 'me and you' time?"

"Sounds great to me," I said. "Let me pop in on the kids and our parents and let them know what's going on. In the meantime, you be thinking about where you'd like to go."

"I can do that," she responded with a big grin.

With that, I projected myself into Brad and Andria's presence, then Lizzie, then the parents to let them know we would be out of circulation for a while. By the time I got back to Jessica, she was beside herself with excitement.

"I'm thinking of a movie title from long ago as our inspiration – 'Around the World in Eighty Days.' We can do that! We can literally circle the globe, stopping at several sites along the way, taking in the local flavor, connecting with the people living in each location, seeing any of the sites we haven't already visited. You know I hear that every local community of Saints has established their own museum of sorts with tributes to many of the Old and New Testament heroes, and even interactive reenactments of many of the Biblical events. We can be a part of the Israeli exodus as the Red Sea is parted, or witness Saul's conversion on the Damascus road, or sit with John as he receives the Patmos revelation. Doesn't all that sound exciting?"

"More than exciting! When do we leave?"

"How about right now? That's another wonderful thing about this trip – no packing and no travel arrangements! We can thought-project part of the trip, fly part of the way, swim part of the way – we might even want to hike through some of the areas just to experience them on a closer level. Oh, and I'd love to go back to the hills of North Carolina. Even with all the challenges of the previous life, we had some wonderful times there. I'd love to revisit the area where we raised our family."

"All right then! Where to first?"

"I've heard there is an area down around the Cape of Good Hope where they're doing some really interesting things in the area of breeding different animals. What say we start there?"

"Sounds good. How do you want to travel this first leg?"

"Let's thought-project. I'm eager to get started!"

With that, we held hands, closed our eyes and opened them on the shores of the Pacific Ocean, just on the outskirts of Cape Town at the tip of the South African continent. We were now in Saint Thomas's area. There had been some effort early on to rename the Cape of Good Hope as the Cape of Saint Thomas, but he had squelched the idea. He had said that it was more of a tribute to live in an area that had a Cape of Good Hope, as it was a reminder of the hope that had now been fulfilled in the reign of Yeshua.

The stories we had heard about what they were doing with the animals was true, but had not prepared us for what we saw. Walking around the area was like walking through a menagerie of the most exotic animals you could ever imagine. Of course, they were all roaming freely. They had no fear of us, and we had nothing to fear from them.

"Ross, look over here!"

Jessica had spotted what at first appeared to be a peacock. Well, I guess it actually was a peacock, but not one like I had ever seen. When it spread its tail feathers, there was an illumination – a rainbow of colors that emanated from its feathers.

"Breathtaking!" I said. "And what is that over there?"

There was a fairly large crowd gathered around what appeared to be horses. As we got closer, we saw that they were winged. They were similar to the horses we had returned on at the end of the tribulation, but we had not seen anything like that bred here on earth until now.

There was a young Mortal – Caleb – who was tending them and answering questions from those gathered around him. We listened as he explained about the breeding process, what they were fed, how they were cared for. Then he said, "Who'd like to go for a ride?"

Every hand went up – including Jessica's and mine! There were ten horses, so it wasn't too long before it was our turn. We climbed aboard, and with just a little nudge, we were off. The horses sprinted about twenty-five yards at a fast gallop – then we were airborne! Sailing out over the Pacific and then back over the peninsula, then out again and around the course where sailing vessels had navigated around the tip of Africa making their trading voyages. It was exhilarating!

When we had landed and thanked Caleb, Jessica said, "Let's try some of the local cuisine."

"Absolutely! You know I'm always up for that."

Each area had developed its own food items, so everywhere you went on the planet there were new tastes to experience. We stayed in Cape Town for several weeks, experiencing the local scenery, many more exotic animals and getting to know some of the residents. Saint Thomas came into town the third week and we had the opportunity to spend some personal time with him. He stayed for the Sabbath Day services that week, which we attended as his guests.

It was a wonderful day of worship. Their praise team led the way, incorporating much of the African culture into their music. After an extended time of lifting up the name of Yeshua, Saint Thomas rose to speak.

"It's wonderful to see many old friends today, and to welcome new ones. You have grown much in number since I was last here. And so much has been accomplished. You are to be commended. As I have told you many times before, you must always remain strong in faith. Never doubt, never waver. The ways of Yeshua are blessed. He is perfect wisdom, perfect love and perfect strength. We live out our days in praise to Him who is worthy of all praise. Praise Yeshua! Praise Yeshua! Praise Yeshua!"

We joined in with the assembled crowd until our voices literally echoed off the mountain ranges. As we did, the Spirit of Yahweh enveloped and filled us until our entire beings were absorbed into His. When we were finally released from the grip of His glory, there was a peace and tranquility that pervaded our very being – a peace that passes all comprehension.

****

The remainder of our trip took us to Madagascar, Sri Lanka, Australia, north to Norway, two stops in old Russia, around to Alaska, down to Toronto, Canada, and finally back to Raleigh, North Carolina. We had been gone for almost three months. Every stop had been full of new wonders, new experiences, and new people to meet and interact with. We had the opportunity to sit down with several of the Saints we had read about in Scripture. Every story had enriched our understanding of Yahweh's dealings throughout the centuries of our previous existence.

Now, as we strolled hand-in-hand through the silence of the wooded hills of our earthly home, there was a different kind of peace.

"I really needed this," Jessica said. "Things had gotten a little difficult back home with all the emphasis on the young people and their questions."

"I know what you mean. I needed this, too. Hey, do you remember the last time we were here?"

"Indeed I do. It was on this very mountainside that you proposed to me. You said you would pledge your love for me to all eternity."

"I did. And I meant it. And here we are – in eternity."

"Well, not quite in eternity – but pretty close!"

We sat and watched the sunset, our nostrils filled with old, familiar fragrances, and our minds filled with old familiar memories.

Then she patted my hand, looked up into my eyes and said, "Time to go home."

We closed our eyes and projected our thoughts back to our home in Salvador. When we opened our eyes, we were home.

CHAPTER 13

"Hey, you guys! It's so good to see you!" Julie was the first to greet us. She had come over to spend some time with Lizzie, and the two of them were sitting out on the deck as we walked up from where we had "landed" down near the river.

"Mom! Dad!" Lizzie came running out to greet us and jumped into my arms. "I've missed you both so much! Even though we were able to track you and talk to you, it's not the same as having you here every day."

"I missed you too, princess," I said. "I think we've got the travel bug out of our system. I don't see us doing that again for quite some time."

"Maybe some shorter trips in the future," Mom said. Lizzie had switched her hug over to her Mom's neck. "And next time you can join us. You'd love so many of the places that we visited."

"Oh, yes, for sure! But for now you have to tell me everything about your trip."

With that, they headed into the house leaving me on the deck with Julie. I sat down next to her in the floating swing.

"And I guess that leaves you to bring me up to date on what's been going on around here. What have you been up to?"

"There's always something new. Brad, Andria and I are very involved with the activities of the praise team. I think they're going to continue into the 3rd Century, KA, but I'm thinking about a change. Bob and Carolyn have really gotten me excited about some of the innovative things they're doing in horticulture, and I'm thinking about joining their team for a while. John and Susan are talking about taking some time off as we enter the new century. The construction projects are interesting, but I think they're ready for a change of pace."

"And what about Lizzie and the grandchildren? How are they doing?"

"Hart and Grace are both doing well. You know it's almost time for them to join in with one of the service teams. Hart is convinced he wants to work in construction, Grace is leaning toward joining one of the praise teams, but they have also talked about doing something where they can share their experiences. They are still almost inseparable. They have some exciting news for you, but I'm going to let them share that personally."

My heart leaped a little bit. I was sure I knew what the news would be. "It is wonderful to see they haven't lost that close connection they had as children. And what about Lizzie?"

Julie glanced over her shoulder to make sure that Lizzie was still in the house with Jessica. "Lizzie is good, Dad. She's the same bundle of joy and energy she was as a child."

"But?" I said.

"But she's not a child any longer. She's approaching the equivalent of sixteen in earth years, and she's actually much more mature than that. Some of that is her own personality, and of course, some of it is due to the extended time she's had to mature here in the Kingdom. She's still very close with Jason, even closer than before you and Mom left on your vacation.

"We rarely get into the conversations that you and the young people were having, but when the subject comes up, it's pretty obvious that Jason hasn't changed his mind about any of his positions. Lizzie tries to reason with him sometimes, but other times she just sits and listens. I've been coming over on a regular basis so that I could have some one-on-one time with her."

"I appreciate that. Maybe we should not have stayed gone for so long."

"Oh, I don't think that's a big issue. Three months in the Kingdom is just a blink. You'll have plenty of time to communicate with her, and with Jason as well. He's here pretty frequently."

With that, Jessica and Lizzie came back onto the deck.

"Oh, Dad," Lizzie said excitedly, "Mom was just telling me about Sri Lanka." She did that sing-songy thing with her voice when she said "Sri Lanka".

"When can I go? When? When? When?"

"We can start making plans right away. When do you want to go? What other plans do you have? Have you thought about what you want to do as far as Kingdom ministry?"

"I have thought about it. I love what Brad and Andria are doing with the praise teams, but Julie's sort of got me excited about the agriculture teams and some of the innovative things that they're into. But alsooo..." Her voice sort of trailed off a bit and she was looking off into the sky. "I'd sort of like to be in whatever group Jason's in, and he's talking about the administrative area."

"Hmmmm," was all I could manage for a moment. "Well, I have a couple of reactions to that. First, I hope Jason – and you – understand that getting into administration at your age means you'll be on the lowest level of the hierarchy. I mean, I hope neither of you think that being in administration is going to mean you're going to have tremendous responsibilities early on."

"Oh, no, Dad. We don't think that at all. We'd just like to be in a position to have some input into policy and procedures."

"Well, that's what I mean. You're not going to be in that position just because you're in administration. At the lower levels, your main responsibilities will be communicating the policies and following up on implementation."

"I understand that, and I'm pretty sure Jason does too. You said you had two reactions?"

"Yes. The second one has to do with your and Jason's relationship. It sounds like you've become quite close."

"It's nothing serious yet." (I'm not sure if she saw me flinch when she said, "yet".) "We just enjoy each other's company. We enjoy talking. He has some very interesting ideas."

"Honey, as I remember some of Jason's 'interesting ideas' they were ones that could lead into some negative – and possibly even dangerous – areas."

She seemed a little shocked. "Really, Dad? Dangerous? What could possibly be dangerous about just discussing ways to make things better?"

My heart was breaking, but I tried to keep an even keel. I looked over to Jessica for support, but her response was to say to Julie, "Why don't you help me in the kitchen? We can start preparing for dinner."

I smiled my "Thanks a lot" smile as they exited.

"Lizzie, you haven't experienced what we did on earth. None of the Mortals has. We lived in a generation where many people thought there was a 'better way.' They rejected Yahweh's plan..."

"Hold on, Dad! No one's talking about rejecting Yahweh or His plan."

"No, not now, not in so many words. But when you say that you're looking for a 'better way' or that you want to change the way things are done, you're implying that there is something wrong or inferior with the way they're being done now. Seriously, Lizzie, look around you. We live in a perfect environment! I hate to keep referring to the 'old days' back before the

Kingdom, but you haven't seen what I've seen. I've seen what happens when humans are in control, when they are free to make the rules, and it's not pretty. I've seen the dark underside of a fallen race, and the pain and heartache that it can cause."

"Dad, I don't even know where all that is coming from. Nobody wants to rebel. Nobody wants to go against the will of Yeshua. I know that He's loving and caring and compassionate, and I know that He has wisdom that we cannot even begin to grasp. And I can't even begin to think of how things could be any better than they already are. But I also think that He gave us minds and creativity and that He expects that we will use them in a positive way."

"You're right, honey. He wants all those things. But He also wants you to trust Him – completely and fully. Trusting Him completely and fully means accepting His word and His way even when we don't totally understand it, even without Him having to give a reason. The heart and the will being totally surrendered to Him is the evidence of spiritual rebirth, and the key to an eternal relationship with Him."

"I know, Dad. You know I do. And I'll get there…and so will Jason."

Before I could respond, Julie poked her head around the corner.

"Don't mean to interrupt, but Mom's considering contacting everyone to have them over for dinner. Is that okay with you, Dad?"

"Sure! I'm always up for an opportunity to see the family. It's been a while since we were all together."

"Oh, Dad," Lizzie said, "Could I invite Jason?"

Apparently, my supernatural abilities did not include the ability to hide disappointment.

"Ok," she said, "never mind."

"Wait, Lizzie, I didn't say 'no'."

"You didn't have to. I saw that look on your face."

"It's just that it's been so long since we had family time. Could we just enjoy one another's company tonight?"

"Sure. No problem." And as she was rounding the corner into the house, "You're the boss."

CHAPTER 14

There was a wonderful time of reuniting as everyone gathered. Even though there was always a sense of connectivity because we were only a thought away, there was still something special about all of us being together physically.

Hart and Grace were the last to arrive. They had planned it that way because they wanted to make an entrance. As soon as they came in, it was obvious. There was a special glow on the faces of those who had fully surrendered to Yeshua. It was almost as if the inner peace radiated through the pores of their skin.

Grace spoke first. "Grandpa, Grandma, we wanted to tell you ourselves. We will be together forever."

"Oh, my babies!" was all Jessica could say as she embraced them both.

It had been some time since I had seen tears on Jessica's cheeks, and even longer since I had felt my own eyes well up with tears. This was truly a red-letter day. There was much hugging and kissing, a lot of congratulations and "Hallelujahs!"

Lizzie participated and smiled and shared in the joy of the moment, but it was obvious that she felt somewhat awkward. With Hart and Grace's conversion, she was the only one in the family that was not assured of eternal life. After a while, I spotted her over at the side of the room and eased over to have a private conversation.

"Well, what about that?" That was my subtle attempt at starting a conversation.

"That's great. I'm really happy for Hart and Grace – for the whole family."

"You know you could make it an even greater day with your own surrender. All the family would be assured of being together forever. With all the goodness we've experienced during the Kingdom Age, eternity promises to be even greater, with more wonders to experience."

"I know, Dad, and you know I'm looking forward to that. I can't bear the thought of ever being separated from you and mom and the rest of the family ever. I just have to get some things worked out in my mind. You know yourself there is plenty of time. We still have over eight hundred years left before the end of the Kingdom Age. There's really no rush, you know."

My heart was breaking. I had heard similar words when I had witnessed to those who were unsaved during the pre-rapture time on earth. Some of them did indeed accept Christ later on in life. But for many of them procrastination became a way of life, until either death came unexpectedly, or their hearts became hardened to the message of the gospel and they died without ever accepting Christ. Many, many more were left behind when the rapture took place, still with the thought that "one day" they would be saved – but that day never came. Instead, they found themselves overwhelmed with the deception of the antichrist, and doomed to an eternity of regret over lost opportunity.

"I know we have eight hundred years left. And I also know that procrastination is seldom a good idea. Resistance strengthens the will to resist. Every day that you wait is one less day you have of enjoying the fullness and peace that comes from knowing that your eternity is secure.

"I love you so much. The only love for you that exceeds my love is the love that Yeshua has for you. The great provision that you are experiencing is only a small example of that love. You don't really understand the concept of suffering, because you've been raised in an environment that does not include suffering. You certainly can't relate to the concept of death. But Yeshua demonstrated His love in the most dramatic way possible. He suffered unimaginable pain, and ultimately gave His life to demonstrate how much He loves us."

"I know, Dad, I know. You had me memorize John 3:16 as soon as I could talk. But..."

"But nothing, Lizzie. I know you know the concept, but you have to look beyond the words and realize what they mean. If Yeshua loved you to the point that He was willing to die, then how could there possibly be any existence better than the one that He has provided? To challenge that, to question whether or not there is some better way of life is to question either His love or His wisdom. You're in effect saying that either there is a better way and He is not aware of it, or He knows of a better way and is withholding it. Either way it casts doubt on His character."

Elizabeth was silent for a few moments, mulling over this perspective.

"Honestly, Dad, I've never looked at it like that. I certainly don't question Yeshua's love or His wisdom. Let me have some time to process. In the meantime, I don't want to take away from the excitement over Hart and Grace's decision and our time together as a family. Let's put this aside for the time being and go enjoy the moment."

"Sounds good. But first, I need – really need – a good Lizzie hug."

We both laughed as we embraced in a big bear hug.

"I love you, honey."

"And I love you, too, Dad. I really, really do."

As we reunited with the rest of the family, all the attention naturally was focused on Hart and Grace. Brad and Andria were just beaming. All of the grandparents were grinning from ear to ear. It was an exciting time for the family and everyone was rejoicing in it.

Lizzie jumped right in. She had always been very close with Hart and Grace and truly shared in their joy and excitement. Things finally settled down enough to sit down to eat.

John stood as we prepared for the blessing.

"Well, to say the least, we have much to be thankful for today. We're two steps closer to having the entire family assured of an eternity together. Let's join hands together as we thank Yeshua for His wonderful provision of eternal life."

CHAPTER 15

Life settled into a satisfying, rewarding routine as we approached the beginning of the Third Century, K.A. Attentions had turned from activity to family. More and more of the Mortals were reaching marrying age and beginning their families. Neither Lizzie nor either of the grandchildren had married yet, but Hart was talking seriously about one particular young lady, and Lizzie was still very close to Jason.

Grace was more focused on her ministry and had not shown any signs of being in any hurry to begin her family. Of course, there was plenty of time. Eight hundred plus years remained in the Kingdom Age, and even the Mortal's bodies never actually grew old, so there was certainly no sense of urgency.

I was sitting out by the lake when Jessica's dad, John, appeared.

"Hello, John. It's good to see you."

"Likewise. Looks like you're enjoying the day."

"Always. This is one of my favorite places. I love the view of the mountains in the background of the lake."

"It is beautiful."

We sat for several minutes just enjoying the view. Finally, he spoke.

"You know I didn't just drop in for the view."

I smiled. John was never one to beat around the bush.

"No, I didn't expect that you had. What's on your mind?"

"You know what's on my mind! Lizzie's on my mind! She's always on my mind. All of those early years – decades – we thought Hart was going to be the one we had to worry about. Now it's Lizzie that's unsaved. What are we going to do?"

"We are going to continue to pray – continue to show her the love of Yeshua – continue to engage her in conversation – continue to answer her questions – and have faith."

"And you think that's enough?"

"What else would you suggest? It's ultimately going to be her choice. We can't force her. Browbeating her is not the answer. Lizzie would never tolerate that. It would just drive her further away. No, love is the answer. Lizzie is smart. She knows the stakes. I believe it's just a matter of time."

"Hrmmph! Just because we live in a different era of time doesn't mean that time has no meaning. There is a limit – even if it is still a long time until the end. And what about Jason? Shouldn't you forbid her to associate with him until he is converted?"

"Forbid her? Lizzie? Are we talking about the same person? You know as well as I do that you don't 'forbid' Lizzie to do anything. She has that stubborn streak she inherited from her mother – you did not hear that from me – and forbidding her to do something is the best way to ensure that she does just exactly that. Besides, I still have hope for Jason. I'm still thinking that as long as Lizzie has a friendship with him, we all have an opportunity to influence him."

"Friendship, huh? That's what you think it is."

"And what do you think it is?"

"I think it's a lot more than friendship. I wouldn't be surprised if he doesn't approach you soon wanting your blessing on a marriage."

I sighed as I gazed back over the lake and up into the mountain ranges. "You're right. I know that. This is the first time I've actually said it out loud."

"You still didn't say it – I did. And what do you intend to do when he does?"

"I honestly don't know. You realize they technically don't need my blessing. They're both adults. They can marry without my blessing, and denying it might drive a wedge between me and Lizzie that would take a long time to repair."

"Well, I suggest you give some serious prayer and consideration to the subject, because I think you're going to have to deal with it sooner rather than later."

We lapsed into another period of silent thought.

After several minutes, John spoke up again.

"Changing the subject, did you hear about what happened yesterday in New Capernaum?"

New Capernaum was a city south of where we lived where John's group had been involved in some new construction.

"No. What happened?"

"There was a Mortal that had been involved in several heated exchanges with one of the Saints in charge of supervision. Apparently, he had been warned several times about challenging the rule of

Yeshua, and each time he just became more adamant in his refusal to cooperate."

"No, I haven't heard anything at all about that. I did not even know that there was resistance on that level. What happened?"

"He was banished."

"He was what?? Banished? What is that?"

"It's the term they are using for the removal of anyone who crosses the line into outright rebellion. Since this incident, I've heard that it's happened a handful of times around the globe. If a person continually resists and rebels to the point that they are not willing to listen, and their rebellion begins to affect others, they are...well, banished. They disappear. We Saints are aware of what has happened, but their memory is erased from the minds of the Mortals and the Adamites. It's as if they never existed. Their souls are assigned to Hell to await the final judgment."

"We were told Yeshua would rule with a rod of iron.[75] I just never knew how His judgment would be carried out."

"Well, now we know. It's decisive and instant. And it's just. We both know what happens if you allow

---

[75] Revelation 2:26-27

sin to take root. It grows and grows, corrupting internally and externally. It's like a cancer in the body that must be excised."

"Oh, I know. I'm not questioning the justice or the necessity. It's just sort of a shock to think about. And it also casts a different light on our perception of how much time we have to win Lizzie...and even Jason. God forbid that they should ever approach that line, that point of no return."

"NO! I'll never accept that possibility. I'm going to double my efforts to try to get through to Lizzie. I'll do anything! I'll sacrifice my own life!"

"John – calm down. I know how you feel. Lizzie is my heart. But Yeshua has already sacrificed His life. There's nothing that you or I can do in that regard that He has not already done. We just have to continue to pray, continue to show her the light. Let's pray right now, and ask for Yeshua's wisdom in how to best approach her."

"You're right, of course. Let's pray."

****

I made a special point of being present the next time that Jason visited.

"Hi, Jason. How have you been?"

"Very good, Mr. Waters. It's good to see you. You haven't been here the last few times I've come by."

"I've been doing some traveling. Jessica and I have been evaluating some ministry opportunities as we enter the Third Century. Lizzie will be down in a bit. Would you like something cold to drink?"

"Sure. If you've got some of that new mango-lime that I had the last time I was here, that would be great."

"I believe we do. Let's go out on the deck and wait for Lizzie."

I got us both a drink and we headed for the deck. I didn't want to waste any time because I did not know when Lizzie would come downstairs, so I dove right in.

"Have you had any more questions since our last discussion? Or maybe you've found some answers?"

"Not too many answers, although I'm coming to realize that some of my questions are pretty shallow. A lot of my lack of ability to accept the answers comes from the lack of perspective that I have. I feel this is pretty common among most of the Mortals. When we hear people talk about pain, suffering, sin and similar topics, we don't really have a frame of reference. We don't even really understand what those words mean. I have thought that if I could experience some of those things it would actually help me."

"Really? That is quite perceptive." My mind was considering a wild idea. "How much have you thought about this? Is this just a passing thought or a serious consideration?"

"No, no – much more than a passing thought. I would love to have some idea of what people are talking about when they discuss those issues."

"Aleph."

I had barely mentioned his name when he appeared before us. Jason was startled to the point he nearly fell off the deck. The appearance of the angels was always somewhat startling, especially to the Mortals. For him to appear suddenly as he did heightened the effect.

Jason recovered somewhat, and was attempting to bow down on one knee when Aleph took his arm and raised him back up.

"Never bow to me. I am but your fellow servant. Yeshua alone is worthy of worship."

"Y..y...es, yes, of course," Jason muttered.

Turning to me Aleph said, "And how may I serve you?"

"I have a question," I said. "Young Mr. Jason has indicated that he would like to experience pain. Is that possible?"

Aleph studied Jason for a moment, looked back at me, then at Jason again.

"If you have his permission, it is possible. Does he know what he is asking?"

"Probably not. But that's the whole point. He cannot relate to things that he has never experienced, and thus is somewhat unable to appreciate their absence. He is also astute enough to recognize that fact."

"As he wishes." And with that, Aleph was gone.

I turned back to Jason. "Are you ready for this?"

"Right now? We're going to do this right now?"

"If it's ok with you, I'm ready."

He took a deep breath as if preparing for a plunge into a pool and said, "All right. Let's go."

Two seconds later, he was writhing on the deck with his hands clutched to his head, screaming in agony. Lizzie had already started down the steps, and at the sound of Jason's screams rushed onto the deck. When she saw Jason on the floor, she started to rush to him, but I stepped between the two of them.

"Dad!" she screamed. "What are you doing? What's wrong with Jason?"

"He'll be all right," I said calmly. "He asked to experience pain."

"But Dad, you've got to make it stop! Make it stop!"

She tried again to go around me to get to him.

"Elizabeth! Step away!"

I don't know if it was my tone or the fact that I had not called her Elizabeth in almost two hundred years, but she stepped back and watched from the side of the room. I noticed a tear roll down her cheek, the first time I had ever seen her cry. This hurt me worse than what Jason was going through.

After approximately two minutes, I reached over and touched Jason's head. Immediately the pain departed and he was left sitting on the floor.

"Wow! That was intense! Are you trying to tell me that what I just experienced was actually a part of your life at one time?"

I smiled as he gathered himself together and sat down in one of the air gliders.

"Jason, what you just experienced was what we on earth called a *headache*. Often times when we would go into a hospital – a place for treating injuries and diseases – they would ask us to rate our pain level on a scale of one to ten. What you just experienced was about a two. I knew you would not be able to handle any more than that."

"No way! You're trying to tell me that there was pain more excruciating than that? How did you cope?"

"In the case of a headache, like you just experienced, we took a couple of aspirin – pain relievers – and went on about our business. Usually it would disappear within a couple of hours – maybe a day at most. But understand what I'm saying to you – to both of you. That little glimpse of pain that you just had would have been a welcome relief to many, many people during our day.

"There were many who experienced levels of pain much greater than that, and had to endure it for years without relief. Most of the population, including my parents, your grandparents, woke up every single day in their later years with pain levels much greater than a headache. Virtually everyone, at several points along their lives, experienced pain at levels nine and ten. Maybe it was after an accident, or maybe after a surgery..."

Jason and Lizzie were looking at me quizzically.

"Yes, I know – you don't really know what either of those terms means either. You've never had an accident, and you've certainly never had surgery. That's the point I'm making. You've never had to endure what I and the other Saints had to endure. And as horrible as the physical pain was for many, that is not the greatest suffering that we experienced."

"What do you mean?" Jason asked. "What could possibly be worse than physical pain of that magnitude?"

"Heartbreak," I replied. "So much deeper and more damaging than any physical pain was the sorrow of a broken heart. To have to watch someone that you loved suffer, to have to say good-by to them as they died; to see your children or someone else that you cared for make horrible decisions that you knew would cause them pain and suffering. The terrible tragedies of violence and war – again words that are foreign to you.

"Violence is acts of harm that people perpetrated against one another, and war is the ultimate violence. It is one nation attacking another, often with millions of lives affected. Our world was involved in warfare almost continually in one area or another. During what we referred to as the Second World War – yes, we were foolish and sinful enough to do it more than once – the majority of the nations of the world were involved in one way or another. Over a six-year period, sixty million people were killed. Forty million of those were not even soldiers. They were civilian casualties, many of them women and children. It's what they called 'collateral damage.'"

By this time, both Lizzie and Jason were in tears.

"Why are you telling us all of this?" Lizzie sobbed. "Why would you want to expose us to those horrible things?"

"Because you need to know in order to understand. All of those things I just described – and many, many more that are even more horrific – came into our world as a result of one thing – sin. You've heard Adam tell his story. He and Eve were placed in an environment just like the one that we live in now. None of those things ever had to happen. One act of disobedience, one simple act of rebellion opened the floodgates of a torrent of sin that ultimately corrupted our entire world.

"And that's why it is so important that we never question the goodness or the wisdom of Yeshua. We must never entertain the thought that He has held back any goodness from us. The simple little thought that Satan planted in the mind of Eve that opened her heart and mind to consider disobedience was this: God hasn't given you His best. He's held back the Tree of the Knowledge of Good and Evil. Why, with that, you become as a god! You'll understand good and evil.[76] You'll be able to choose for yourself how to live your life. And so they did. Six thousand years of pain and suffering and evil later, Yeshua has redeemed us and restored us. We must never go down that trail again."

"Of course not," Jason said, still weeping openly. "Yeshua's way is the one and only way. I will never again question it."

"Nor will I," Lizzie said.

At that instant, they were both granted the gift of eternal life!

---

[76] Genesis 3:5

CHAPTER 16

We entered into the Third Century K.A. on a spiritual high. All of the immediate family was now secured for eternity. There would never be another time of separation.

As expected, Jason and Lizzie came to me shortly after the turn of the century and asked for my blessings on their marriage – which I enthusiastically granted. Two years later Hart was married to a beautiful young Asian Mortal – Yang Sun. Five years into the Third Century, Grace was married to a young Mortal whose parents had been missionaries to Peru during their time on earth. She became Mrs. Zach Golden in a beautiful ceremony held at the site of Zach's parent's mission church in Peru.

And so began the next cycle of our lives in the Kingdom.

We had already been here for over two hundred years, the equivalent of almost three earth lifetimes. We had traveled over the world – although there were still many places we had not seen. We had experienced joys and pleasures that had once been unimaginable. We often reflected on the Scripture where we had been told that the wonders that awaited us were beyond our ability to even imagine them:

"Eye has not seen, nor ear heard, neither hath entered into the heart of man, the things which God hath prepared for them that love Him."[77]

How often I used to quote that verse, then let my imagination run wild with expectation. But it was true. I could not imagine it. I could not conceive in my mind the wonders of Yahweh's creativity and love.

Still almost eight more centuries lay ahead – nearly eight hundred more years of wonder and discovery and unbridled joy.

"Hey, Dad."

Brad's voice startled me a little. I realized that I had been daydreaming, caught up in the wonder of the moment.

"Hi, Son. What's up?"

"Not much. I had some free time and wanted to catch up on things. We've been occupied for a while with wedding plans and getting Grace and Zach situated and haven't had a lot of time to just talk."

I couldn't help but smile. Brad and I had a good relationship when he was growing up. We had our moments, as all fathers and sons did, but we always

---

[77] I Corinthians 2:9

enjoyed an easy camaraderie and treasured our time together.

"You looked like you were a million miles away when I came up. What were you thinking about?"

"I guess you could say I was in review mode," I said. "I was looking back over the last two hundred years and thinking about the wonders we had seen, the glorious blessings we have enjoyed. You know, I used to think a lot about this time, back in the pre-rapture days. I would try to imagine how wonderful it would be...but even now, it's hard to believe all that we have been given."

"Man, I know what you mean. It really is surreal on a certain level. Sometimes when I wake up, it takes a moment to realize that I'm really here, that this is not just a fantastic dream. And to think that whenever we were alive on earth, there were times that I hoped that the Lord would delay His coming."

"Really? You never told me that."

"Of course not! I couldn't tell my pastor dad that I didn't want the Lord to return. But there was an earthly mindset that said, 'I want to see my children grow up. I want to have grandchildren. I want to do this or that.' It never really clicked with me that the Kingdom Age would provide the opportunity for all those things, and do so in an environment that is so much better – infinitely better. No crime; no disease; no negative influences of any kind; no worries about finances or schedules. On top of that, the slowing down of the aging process meant that I was able to enjoy each stage of my children's lives for ten times longer than I would have before. It's pretty awesome."

"It is that. Now you get to really start having fun! With Hart and Grace both married now, you'll soon become a grandpa."

"And so will you, with Lizzie and Jason. How about that? We're going to become grandpas together!"

That thought made both of us laugh out loud.

"Indeed we will!" I said. "We'll have to get together and compare notes, although you know I have much more experience, having already been grandpa to Hart and Grace."

"Right. How about - you bring the experience and I'll bring the fresh, new outlook?"

"Sounds like an unbeatable team to me, son. I can hardly wait."

Changing the subject, Brad asked, "When's our next family outing?"

"Your mom and I were just talking about that. We'd like to do it in the next few weeks, and we're thinking about something out near the Hawaiian Islands. In addition to all the natural beauty, that is part of Simon Peter's territory. I understand the people there have constructed a colossal tribute to the life of Yeshua on earth. They are using holographic images of Yeshua and all the apostles to allow you to experience first-hand what it would have been like to walk with Him. You see the miracles, hear His teaching...it's supposed to be very moving. If you choose, you can actually walk with Him in 'real time' through the entire three and a half years of His earthly ministry. It's one of the perks that come from having centuries of time at your disposal."

"Sounds great! Of course, count us in. Just let us know the dates. This will be the first family get-together we've had since the family has grown. We'll have to sit three more places at the table this time."

"Well, two more, anyway. Jason had already sort of become a part of the family even before he and Lizzie got married."

"True. I know you were a little worried there for a while. Jason seemed to be resisting Yeshua's reign, and

I know you were concerned about the impact that would have on Lizzie."

"I don't know if I'd say 'resisting'. I prefer to say 'questioning'. But, yes, I was concerned and made it a matter of much prayer. Of course, there are still some of the Mortals who are yet unsaved. We must continue to pray for them and try to show them the truth. Part of the challenge we face in the next generation is that we will have children who will be raised by uncommitted parents. Although no overt rebellion will be tolerated, there is always what we used to call the 'generational drift.' Children tend to be less committed than their parents, who in turn were often less committed than the grandparents, and so on."

"I have not thought about that," Brad said. "But I can certainly see it. If the parents are not totally committed to the precepts of the reign of Yeshua, they will be less likely to impress upon their children their importance, and more likely to entertain ideas that might one day be the seeds of rebellion."

"Exactly. And we 'grandpas' are going to have to be even more diligent to share our faith with our grandchildren, knowing that there will be those voices of dissent attempting to lure them off the path."

"We can be each other's accountability partners," Brad laughed.

"Indeed we can, son. Indeed, we can. Now, what do you say we go see what the ladies are up to? I smell something good coming from the kitchen."

CHAPTER 17

"Oh, aren't they just precious? I could just eat them up!"

Carolyn's words expressed all our feelings and were greeted with choruses of "Amen!" and "Oh, yes!" from all the family.

We had all gathered – the whole clan – for the birth of Hart and Yang's twins. The twin gene had obviously been passed down from Hart, and the result was two beautiful twin girls. Their mother's olive complexion and Hart's striking blue eyes made for an almost hypnotizing beauty – or so it seemed to the proud parents, grandparents, great-grandparents and the extended family.

This was the culmination of a wave of new arrivals that had started with the birth of Jason and Elizabeth's son, JJ – short for Jonathon Jason, who had been born in K.A. 208. Grace and Zach had a little girl in K.A. 210 – Sue Ann, named after Jessica's mom. Jason and Elizabeth had followed up with a girl of their own in K.A. 211, Jewel. Now here we were in K.A. 214 with twin girls.

Life was good! Even in the pre-rapture era, the birth of children and grandchildren was always a time of excitement and joy. Far too often, those times were marred by either disease or other complications, or at least the potential for bad things. Not so here. There was nothing to distract from the pure joy of new life. No fears or concerns to dull the edge of the excitement. There was always much rejoicing and usually an extended time of celebration surrounding the birth of any child. That would certainly be the case for the Waters family!

Yang had barely gotten settled in with the twins when she started getting peppered with requests to hold them, and of course, the always important question – "What are you going to name them?"

Hart looked down at Yang as if to say, "This is your show."

"We have chosen two great characters of the Bible to honor. Deborah[78] was one of the great judges of Israel, and Ruth[79] was the wife of Boaz and an ancestor of Yeshua. Deborah and Ruth."

"Perfect," I said. "I can't wait to share with them the stories of their namesakes."

"I'm afraid you're going to have to get in line for that," Hart said, grinning from ear to ear. "Dad's get first dibs on the story telling."

---

[78] Judges 4:4
[79] Ruth 4:13, 21-22

"As it should be," Bob said. "Ross always claimed that privilege."

"OK, OK, I get it. Don't start ganging up on me. I yield to father's rights," I said, bowing graciously to Hart and Yang.

"I think it's time to get the party started," Brad chimed in. "There's a table load of food out there that's calling my name."

"Indeed," said John. "But first, a prayer of thanks and praise for two more wonderful additions to the Waters family."

With heads bowed we all joined our hearts and voices in praise to Yeshua for the great gift of life, for the blessed provision of a perfect environment in which to raise our young ones, and for the prospects of a future filled with joy, happiness and adventure.

****

The next one hundred years were the best we had experienced to date – and that is saying something. The environment, of course, remained the epitome of excellence. Free from the concerns over our children that had cast a shadow over some of the earlier decades, the family reveled in our enjoyment of one another. Our experience was representative of all the families of the earth.

The attention of much of the population had turned from a focus on the various areas of production to enjoying relationships with their families. Not that there was not still production going on, but so much technology had been developed that there was minimal need for human involvement. Food could be produced much faster than it could be consumed. There was still construction taking place, but there was never any need to replace existing construction because it just did not deteriorate. There was still innovation and creativity taking place, yet even that had slowed as the boundaries of what was possible were approached.

In the pre-rapture earth, there was often much grieving over the death of a loved one, especially if they died at a young age. There was always the feeling that so much had been missed, so many opportunities that you would never get to experience. The Kingdom banished all those regrets. Time and experiences on earth paled in comparison to what was available now. There were no concerns whatsoever about safety or travel. Finances were not even a consideration, because everything was free! The length of time available to enjoy each stage of life was multiplied tenfold.

In addition, there were opportunities available now that were unavailable during our earthly existences. Worldwide travel was commonplace. In addition, there were several orbiting space stations that offered spectacular views of the earth and the galaxy that were available for anything from family vacations to afternoon luncheons. Visits to these were as common as a trip to the mall had been.

In addition, there was the aspect of the righteousness and justice of the kingdom. *"With righteousness shall He judge the poor, and reprove with equity for the meek of the earth."*[80]

A world of perfect equity, perfect justice, and the Word of the Lord is the supreme law of the land. There are no riots, no demonstrations. No crime, no injustice. No bigotry, no betrayal. Nothing but pure joy, reveling in the goodness and grace of Yeshua.

Who could possibly want anything more?

---

[80] Isaiah 11:4

CHAPTER 18

We decided to celebrate the turn of the 4th Century K.A. by having our family get-together on one of the orbiting space stations. The Saints were able to project ourselves there, or even chose a form that would allow us to fly. However, those not in glorified bodies needed transportation, and for those, multiple shuttles left on an hourly basis from spots all over the planet. The individual shuttles would seat one thousand passengers each.

We chose to all ride together in one of the shuttles, just so that we could enjoy the trip together. We had decided to meet at the shuttle station in Cape Canaveral, Florida. With its long and storied history of rocket and shuttle launches, it had seemed only appropriate to use it as one of the terminals for the current shuttle program.

"Grandpa!"

Sue Ann's squeal of delight alerted the other grandchildren and sent them all scurrying toward Jessica and me as we arrived at the station.

"Come here, you little rascals. Give me a hug."

The youngsters were all approaching the equivalent of ten years old, although they had been alive for almost a hundred years. They were all bundles of boundless energy and joy, and they seemed to have an endless capacity for love. The joy we had experienced over the last century can hardly be put into words.

After much hugging and kissing, we finally got around to greeting the other adults. Ours had become quite the entourage. When everyone was present – as was the case today – there were now twenty of us in all.

"Hey, Dad," said Brad. "We were beginning to think you and mom weren't going to make it."

"You're joking, right? No way I'd miss a gathering of the clan. We took a little side trip to pick up something for the kids. Hey, kids! Go see what Grandma has for you!"

This started a stampede toward Jessica.

"Hold on! Hold on!" she chided them. "We have something for everyone."

"You know you're going to spoil them, don't you?" Lizzie said, complaining a little, but all the while grinning from ear to ear.

"Of course I do! That's what Grandpas do. And by the way, I did a little spoiling of you growing up, too, if you remember, and I think you turned out all right."

"That's up for debate," Hart teased.

Lizzie responded with a playful punch to the shoulder.

I started trying to make my way around to the others. "Bob, Carolyn, it's good to see you, as always. And John – it's been almost a year since we've seen you and Susan."

"It has been," John said. "Susan and I have been traveling. I can't wait to tell you about some of our adventures."

"Hart, Yang, come here, you two! Are you still enjoying your new home in Costa Rica? It is a beautiful place."

"It is indeed," Yang said. "And yes, every day is still full of indescribable joy – 'joy unspeakable' – to use the Biblical terminology. You saw the waterfall in front of the house when you came to visit. Debbie and Ruth have both taken to kayaking over the falls and cliff diving from the rocks into the pool at the base of the waterfall."

The amazing part of that revelation is that no one blinked an eye. In our previous existence, there would have been gasps of shock and amazement, if not anger, that ten year olds would be allowed to engage in such activity. Here, there was no danger. There was no risk. The perfection of their bodies meant that they were physically capable of amazing feats. Even if some mishap were to occur, the angels were always present, always vigilant.

"...He shall give His angels charge over thee, to keep thee in all thy ways. They shall bear thee up in their hands, lest thou dash thy foot against a stone."[81]

So the conversations proceeded as if she had said they had taken up rock collecting.

"Julie! How's my girl?"

"Wonderful, dad. Actually better than wonderful. I have some exciting news for everyone."

This got everyone's attention as they all circled around Julie to hear. She took a deep breath before proceeding.

"As perfect as this environment is, there have been certain aspects of it I have not been able to actively participate in. Since Roger was an unbeliever

---

[81] Psalm 91:11-12

and we had never had any children, I have not had the joy that the rest of the family has shared in raising and experiencing the love of children. Well; I've met someone. His name is Will. He was saved as a young child and translated during the rapture. Unfortunately, his wife was unsaved.

"They did, however, have a two year old daughter who was translated with her father. She, of course, has grown up in the Kingdom, given her commitment to Yeshua, married and had two children. They also have grown up, both committed to Yeshua and each have a child of their own – one is a toddler, about ten years old, and the other is an infant. Will has asked me to partner with him in the raising of the children, to be sort of a substitute grandma."

Julie was literally beaming.

"Oh, Julie," Jessica said. "That's wonderful! I am so happy for you!"

The whole family collapsed on her, hugging, kissing, crying.

Finally Bob said, "And when do we get to meet Will and the family?"

"Soon," Julie said. "There's no way I would have brought him to a family outing unannounced, but very soon."

The announcement from the flight control center interrupted our celebration.

"Now boarding flight number 743 to Space Station Petra. All passengers on flight 743 report to Gate 82. The flight is scheduled for departure in fifteen minutes."

"That's us," John said. "We had better make our way to the gate. But first, how about a great big 'hallelujah'?"

Our praise echoed through the terminal, and was actually joined with choruses of hallelujah from the crowd. Praise to Yeshua was a common thing, and a shared experience by all, even if they didn't know the specific nature of the praise.

"All I can say is, this is going to be one memorable outing," Brad said.

"For sure," Julie said. "Right now, we'd better head to the shuttle. We don't want to miss our flight."

The shuttle ride itself was always a treat for the kids, no matter how many times they had taken it. The views from the shuttle were always spectacular. Yeshua would often dazzle with His own version of a fireworks show. Meteor showers and the occasional explosion of a distant star were always wonders to anticipate. If your timing was right, you could get a view of the earth rising above the surface of the moon. A picture of this had been taken by one of the astronauts on the Apollo 8 mission. At the time, it was an iconic photo, and it was still a very impressive sight. Of course, there were the actual views of earth itself. The children never tired of identifying land masses and bodies of water from space.

The ride itself took about an hour, and of course, there was a lot of conversation among the adults, most of it centered on Julie's new relationship.

"OK," I said, once we had gotten the kids seated on the shuttle. "I want to know everything."

"We all do!" Jessica added.

Julie took a deep breath and began.

"As I said, Will was saved as a child. His parents died when he was young, both unsaved. He was adopted and raised in a Christian home, and it was through that experience that he came to know Christ at Vacation Bible School. There was a time in his teenage years that he came to resent the fact that God had taken his parents, although now he clearly sees that if it were not for that, he probably would never have become a Christian.

"Because of that resentment, he wandered away from the church when he was old enough to leave home, and married someone who was not a Christian.

Later in life, he repented and returned to Christ and the church, but his wife was never comfortable with it. She divorced him after three years and went her separate way. Obviously, she never came to Christ, because she is not here. He says the only good thing to come out of that relationship was their daughter, Carla.

"As I said before, Carla is committed to Yeshua, and is married to a son of a missionary family. His name is Paul – of course – and they have two children. There's Meghan, who will turn ten in a couple of months, so about one in earth years. Can't wait for you to meet her. She's a charmer. And then there's Paul, Jr., whom they call PJ, who was born 4 months ago."

"You haven't told us how you met Will," Hart said.

"Oh, yes," Julie continued. "Will was on the praise team with us last year."

Hart turned to Grace and said, "See, I told you it was that Will." Then to Julie, "I told her there was some chemistry between you two, but she said I was imagining it."

"OK, OK, so you were right," Grace conceded.

"Anyway," Julie went on, "we maintained contact over the next few years and became friends. It has only been over the last few months that it has developed into a closer relationship. I didn't really want to say anything until I saw where it was headed. He asked last week if I would consider becoming a part of their family – and I agreed!"

"That is wonderful news!" I said. "I can't wait to meet them and get to know them."

The discussion continued for the remainder of the flight, sometimes drifting off onto other topics, sometimes taking in the splendor of our majestic surroundings, until the announcement from the Captain signaled our arrival.

"Ladies and gentlemen, thank you for flying with us. Your flight will dock in seven minutes. We hope you enjoy your visit."

As we disembarked, the sign that greeted us above the entrance to the space station said it all:

*"The heavens declare the glory of the Lord,
and the firmament shows His handiwork."*[82]

---

[82] Psalm 19:1

CHAPTER 19

The next five hundred years – yes, I said five hundred years – brought wave after wave of new enjoyments and experiences. It would take thousands of volumes to describe each one in detail.

Before I proceed, a moment of reflection.

I and the rest of the Saints, along with those who entered the Kingdom at the onset, had lived in this unimaginably perfect place now for over nine hundred years. NINE HUNDRED YEARS! Four times as long as the United States existed as a nation! The equivalent of over 13 seventy-year life cycles! I say this so that you don't lose perspective. This short recap of our lives during the Kingdom Age is just that – a short recap. Even as we approach the close of this era, and anticipate what was to come, it has been an immensely fulfilling experience.

Our family continued to grow. The addition of Will and his family brought our number to twenty-five – and we were just getting started! Jason and Lizzie had three more children, two boys and a girl. Hart and Yang had four more children, three girls and a boy. Grace Zach had three more children, including a set of twin boys and another daughter. And Carla and Paul had two more daughters.

Then began the generational multiplication. By the end of the 6th Century K.A., our youngsters who had grown and married had produced seventy-six offspring. By the end of the 8th Century K.A., they had produced a whopping three hundred and seventy-one. Needless to say, the family get-togethers were now mammoth events with our total number now exceeding five hundred. It was rare that we could all get together at the same time, so we often broke the group down into branches of the families to allow for a little more individual interaction. There were also constant opportunities to build relationships on more intimate levels. Groups of the family often travelled together and the youngsters were always involved in similar activities that kept them connected.

Two things did change as we neared the end of this fantastic era.

After the close of the 8th Century, there were no more children born – not just in our family, but also worldwide. The Saints all understood the reasoning behind Yeshua's ban, and we tried as best as we could to communicate it to the others.

As we approached the end of the Kingdom Age, we knew what was going to happen. Lucifer, bound and restrained for the length of the Millennial, was about to be freed. His goal would be to identify those who had not yet committed to Yeshua and attempt to deceive them into following him in an uprising. The reason for no children born after the beginning of the 8th Century is that there must be no one who, by virtue of age, had not had the opportunity to experience the goodness of Yeshua, and be mature enough to choose to commit their lives totally to Him. This was the only way to avoid the great deception.

The second change is somewhat related to the first. As we approached the day that Satan would be released, the evidences of rebellion became more and more evident. We had watched as the centuries had gone by a gradual decline in commitments to Yeshua in each succeeding generation. We had begun to see pockets of resistance to the rule of Yeshua.

Of course, no outright rebellion was tolerated. However, there were those who exhibited a type of passive resistance, such as refusing to go up to Jerusalem as proscribed for the Feast of Tabernacles. The Bible had prophesied about those groups. In those areas where this occurred, the rainfall needed for their crops was withheld until they complied.[83] No one went hungry, of course. There was always food available from neighboring communities, but there was a stigma attached to the understanding that resistance to the will of Yeshua had brought the judgment. And, sadly, there were increasingly more banishments every year.

---

[83] Zechariah 14:16-19

Even though we hated to witness this tragedy, we somewhat understood its causes.

As the generations progressed, more and more children were born to parents who themselves were not committed. Thus, they failed in their own parental responsibilities to bring up their children in the love and reverence for the Lord. Even though there were Godly influences abounding, the lack of a strong reinforcement at home left many of these children vulnerable.

Another contributing influence is that we were now almost a thousand years removed from any negative experiences at all. The generations that had been born since the beginning of the Kingdom Age had never experienced any deprival or disappointment of any kind whatsoever. When we tried to tell the younger generations about the day that was coming when Lucifer would be released and there would be an attempt to unseal Yeshua, there would be one of three reactions.

Fortunately, the most common of the three was belief and commitment to Yeshua. The vast majority of the world's twenty-eight billion inhabitants were committed followers of Yeshua. And why not? His goodness, His grace, His power, and His justice had been on public display for almost a thousand years.

The second response was disbelief. There were those who simply could not comprehend such a drastic change to the only environment they had ever known. They viewed the stories as some type of myth made up by the Saints to keep everyone in line. How familiar this response sounded! We had heard the same one back on the earth in the days prior to the Rapture. No matter how fervently we had tried to warn them, a huge percentage of the population at that time – even many professing Christians – never took seriously the message of the imminent return of the Lord.

The third response is the hardest for me to comprehend. There were some who were still of the mindset that somehow the reign of Yeshua was oppressive. They were the passive resisters, the perpetually dissatisfied. I had heard it all before.

"If only I could make my own choices. Why does there have to be so many rules? How is it that you Saints get glorified bodies and no one else does?" It was the soil of discontent that would make them fertile ground for the deceptive message of the enemy.

The unbelievers and the malcontents made up an extremely small percentage of the population, less than one-half of one percent. But with a global population of over twenty-eight billion, that still represented over a hundred and forty million people. No wonder John the

Revelator described the number participating in the rebellion to be as "the sand of the sea."[84]

My heart breaks when I consider that three of my own descendents were still uncommitted. They were all of the last generation. I kept thinking that if only there were more time. The last generation would be the one with the least amount of time to decide. Again, it had unfolded that way on earth. There were so many of that last generation that were caught unprepared because "they had plenty of time." They never consciously rejected the message of the gospel, they just procrastinated.

"Someday, one day…" became the tool of Satan to seal their eternal fate, because for so many, "someday" never came.

Of course, we did everything we could. We reasoned, we cajoled, we begged. For the ones who were willing, we even took them down the route that I had taken Jason. But for many, the response was not one of comprehension and reflection on all that they had been spared. Instead, it produced bitterness and resentment, as though I were trying to torture them into accepting my way of thinking.

It was tragic and heart wrenching to watch as we got closer and closer to the time of the rebellion,

---

[84] Revelation 20:8

knowing the destruction that awaited all of those who would participate. A destruction that would not only bring an end to their earthly existence, but would carry forward into eternity as well.

THE FINAL CHAPTER

As we neared the end of the Kingdom Age, our family gatherings had lost some of their jovial nature. We were always glad to reconnect and to see all the members of the family, but we knew what was on the horizon. We had all read the prophecy of John. For that matter, we had all heard him share the message personally. The closing days of earth's golden age would end in one final battle – if you could call it that. There would be an assault on Jerusalem, led by Satan himself, with the goal of unseating Yeshua.

We had chosen Egypt as the site of what would be our last family get-together prior to the end of the Kingdom Age. Although we did not know the exact timing, or how it would go down, we wanted to be in the area of Jerusalem to show our support for Yeshua.

Julie found me sitting out on the banks of the Nile River.

"Hi, dad. May I join you?"

"You know you never have to ask that. You're as welcome in my arms today as you were that first day at the hospital. You were the most beautiful thing I had ever seen. You have been my joy ever since."

"Stop it, Dad! You always could make me cry."

"Not my intent, honey. Come here and sit beside me."

For some time, we relived our lives together. It had been a while since we had used the ability we had as Saints to project ourselves into different life situations. Now it seemed so appropriate.

First, she was a baby snuggling in my arms. Then a precocious infant, charming me in a way that no one else could. Then as she grew, I taught her how to ride a bike, and she taught me how to love unconditionally. Next, a blossoming teenager, full of energy and curiosity – oh, how many times that curiosity landed her in hot water. Finally, a beautiful young lady - mature, confident, so capable. The Kingdom Age had been every father's dreams about an ongoing relationship with his daughter.

After several hours of this marvelous interaction, Julie said, "What a wonderful life we've had. Even on earth, I always knew how blessed I was. And the Kingdom Age has been more than I could have ever dreamed. Have you thought much about what happens next?"

"As a matter of fact, that's what I was thinking about when you came. You know there are some dark times ahead. It's going to be traumatic for everyone, but more for some than others."

"How so?"

"It will be more difficult for the Adamites and the Mortals than for the Saints. They have never experienced anything like what is coming. We at least have some frame of reference. We saw devastation and death in the previous life, and we witnessed the Battle of Armageddon. We've seen at least a taste of the carnage that is coming at the final battle. For those who have never witnessed it, it will be like getting your first taste of water by being submerged in a hundred foot deep river.

"And it will be extremely hard on those who have loved ones who are part of the rebellion. We will share in that sorrow, but it will be magnified the closer you are to the individual. Many will have to watch sons and daughters, brothers and sisters, even parents, chose a path that will lead to their destruction.

"And if that were not enough, the Great White Throne Judgment[85] is to follow. Billions will be called out of Hell to stand before Yeshua. From the very first rebel who ever lived and died, to the last one to perish in the final rebellion, they will all stand before the throne."

I turned to see her crying.

---

[85] Revelation 20:11-15

"Oh, sweetie, I'm sorry. I didn't mean to upset you."

"No, dad, it's ok. I know all of this, have known it my whole life. You made sure of that. Thank you so much for that, by the way. I was just thinking of how it would be to see Roger there. I hate it so that he missed all of this because of his stubbornness. I'm not looking forward to the moment when he stands in judgment."

"Of course you're not. None of us are. There will be a lot of weeping there. It is not until after the Great White Throne that we are promised that He will wipe every tear from our eyes, and there will be no more sorrow.[86]"

"Do you know how He'll do that? Remove all the sorrow for those who have rejected?"

"I've heard it said that He will remove that which causes the sorrow. Some have speculated that to mean He will remove them from our memory, along with every other negative memory of our previous existence. I guess we'll have to wait and see. It won't be long now."

****

The release of Satan was not at all what I had imagined. In my mind, there would be a huge hole that

---

[86] Revelation 21:4

would appear, and he would emerge, hissing and fuming, shouting blasphemies and brandishing a pitchfork. It was nothing like that at all. In fact, most of the world was not even aware that he had been released.

He appeared on the scene one day – not as the demonic figure that we had seen when he had been cast into the bottomless pit – but rather in the guise he had assumed as the antichrist. Suave and charismatic, with a speech that both captivated and hypnotized.

His message was just what the rebels had been waiting to hear. Finally, someone with the courage to say what they had all been thinking. Why should Yeshua get to make all the decisions? Were they not creatures of free will? Could they not have some say in how they were to be governed?

Voices of protest that only a few days earlier would have resulted in banishment were allowed to be heard. The more they were heard, the more followers they attracted. Over the course of a few months, demonstrations had begun in cities around the world. The local judges wanted to intervene, but Yeshua prohibited it. The final chapter of the story was being played out.

The strategy was developed and communicated. As time approached for the next Feast of Tabernacles, they would gather in Jerusalem. How ironic that so many who had shown their contempt for the rule of Yeshua by refusing to come at the appointed time would choose to express their rebellion by making this journey. Somehow, to them, it seemed fitting.

The plan was simple enough. No one was foolish enough to think that they could overcome Yeshua by force. But surely, when He saw so many of His subjects upset and wanting change, He would listen. He would hear their complaints. He would accommodate their requests, no, their demands. Then they would set up a separate nation, with their new leader enthroned, and they would live life as they chose. Never again would they be subject to the law of Yeshua.

The massive crowd surrounded the city of Jerusalem, taking several weeks to assemble. Each passing day, Satan was at work, stirring up emotions, whipping them into a frenzy. By the time they all had gathered, the objective had changed dramatically. Satan had convinced them that they actually had a number large enough to dethrone Yeshua. They did not have to settle for a separate country. They could rule the world! Manifesting himself now in an image of power and splendor, his spell over them was complete. He would make them all gods! They themselves would reign.

It was not pretty. It ended almost before it began.

When the first wave of assault moved toward the throne, the heavens opened and a rain of fire and brimstone descended on the assembled masses.[87] I would say that they were fortunate that it ended so quickly, except that the next moment they found themselves in the pits of hell to await their soon coming day of judgment. Some failed to even recognize that they had been destroyed; such was the similarity between their last moments on earth and their first moments in eternity.

Lucifer had now taken on his demonic form and attempted one last charge at the throne. He was snatched by Yeshua's power, and without so much as a comment from Yeshua, the enemy of Christ and His church was hurled into the lake of fire, to join the false prophet and the antichrist who had been incarcerated there one thousand years earlier,[88] and to await the billions that would soon join them after the Great White Throne.

The epic event that would follow was like nothing ever witnessed. It transpired above the earth's stratosphere, but was clearly visible to all who were still on the earth. It was as if it were projected on the theater screen of the sky.

---

87 Revelation 20:7-9
88 Revelation 20:10

Every soul that had ever lived, in every era of time, who had not accepted the blood of the Lamb of God as payment for their sins were gathered before the throne. The most evil men and women of history were there. The tyrants, the butchers, the murderers, the rapists, the drug dealers. Standing right alongside them were many that the world had admired and held in high esteem. The philanthropist, the teacher, the soldier, the police officer, the stay-at-home mom.

They all had one thing in common. When asked, "What will you do with My Son?" they had given the wrong answer. Many tried to hide, but there was no place to hide. They tried to escape, but there was no place to run.

Those of us who had experienced the Judgment Seat of Christ knew what was happening. In each person's mind, his or her life was being reviewed. Every evil deed. Every idle word. Every instance of rebellion. Along with each opportunity they had been given to receive the gospel, or at least to open themselves to the evidences of creation and conscience. All of this had been recorded in what John had called "the books."[89] As it turns out, "the books" were their own memories. Locked inside the recesses of their minds were the details of every instance of their lives.

[89] Revelation 20:12

If you focused on individual faces, you could see the agony. Some of the more proud started out with looks of defiance, but that did not last very long. Confronted with their sin and their rejection of the light, they would all come to accept that the judgment that was coming had been earned. One by one, they dropped to their knees.

"Wherefore God also has highly exalted Him, and given Him a name which is above every name: that at the name of Jesus every knee should bow, of things in Heaven, and things in earth, and things under the earth; and that every tongue should confess that Jesus Christ is Lord, to the glory of God the Father."[90]

A final proclamation was made. As evidence of their failure to accept salvation, it was confirmed that indeed their names were not written in the Lamb's Book of Life.[91]

Then, it was over. The final banishment of every rebel to the lake of fire. Eternal torment awaited them. Even as they disappeared, their memories began to fade from our consciousness.

---

[90] Philippians 2:9-11
[91] Revelation 20:15

EPILOGUE

The close of the Kingdom Age signaled the beginning of the Eternal Day. It began in the most spectacular way imaginable.

John had said it simply: *"And I saw a new heaven and a new earth: for the first heaven and the first earth were passed away; and there was no more sea."*[92]

Peter was a little more graphic. *"But the day of the Lord will come as a thief in the night; in the which the heavens shall pass away with a great noise, and the elements shall melt with fervent heat, the earth also and the works that are therein shall be burned up."*[93]

It was a stunning display. With all of the believers safely secluded in a protective bubble in outer space, we watched as the universe exploded around us. There has never been a fireworks display approaching this. From every corner of the universe, galaxies were ablaze. We watched as the closer planets and heavenly bodies – including our man-made space stations – seemed to melt and then evaporate. Every vestige of the original creation, with the exception of humans themselves, was eliminated.

---

[92] Revelation 21:1
[93] II Peter 3:10

And then, the real show began.

Moses had stated it so simply in Genesis, possibly because he had not been there to witness it. *"In the beginning, God created the heaven and the earth."*[94]

Yeshua's power had been on display before. Moses had watched Him part the Red Sea.[95] Joshua had seen Him cause the sun to stand still in the sky.[96] The disciples and followers of the New Testament had watched Him heal the sick, command the wind and the sea, cast out demons, and even raise the dead.

No one had ever seen anything like this.

With the power of His spoken word, He recreated the universe. He created the stars in the palm of His hand and then flung them to the far reaches of space, each one leaving a trail of sparkling fire as they expanded to enormous sizes before reaching the place of their preordained positions. He spun the planets and their moons from His hand into their respective orbits.

Finally, He turned to our own solar system, this time with only the earth hanging in the emptiness of space. There was no sun created for our planet. John had said we would not need one. Indeed, we did not.

---

[94] Genesis 1:1
[95] Exodus 14:21
[96] Joshua 10:12-13

The brilliant glory of Yeshua enveloped the planet, creating one eternal day. We did not realize it at the time, but every planet He recreated was now inhabitable, and would one day be populated by His children.

We returned to the newly created earth at this point. As perfect as we had thought our environment to be before, this was even more pristine. Everything was washed, everything was clean. There was not a taint of sin or corruption to be found anywhere in this new universe.

As we stood in amazement, we beheld the crown jewel of His creation – the New Jerusalem, the City of God![97]

I guess John had done his best, with the vocabulary he had available to him to attempt a description. But oh, how short he had fallen! I fear I will do no better.

The first thing that strikes you is the brilliance. It shines like a small sun, yet somehow the brightness does not cause you to shield your eyes or turn away. Instead, it is as if it envelops you. It was the same sensation I had when the church was caught up, when I saw the glory of Yeshua and yet was not overcome by it. No wonder –

---

[97] Revelation 21:9-27

the brightness of the city comes from the glory of the Godhead!

As it got closer, the second thing I noticed was its size. It was immense! I didn't notice it at first, because my first glimpse was from several hundred miles away. But as it got closer and closer, it became obvious that this was the size of a small moon! Shaped similar to a giant cube, the height, breadth, and width were all equal – 1,500 miles on each side and top to bottom.[98]

Interestingly, most Christians on earth had gotten their concept of what Heaven would be like from John's description of this city. Gates of pearl. Streets of gold. Walls of jasper. The throne with the River of Life flowing from it. The jewel encrusted walls. Check, check, check. They were all there.

The most striking part to me was the refraction of the light of His glory as it shone through the streets of translucent gold and reflected off the multi-colored jewels. Walking inside the city is like walking in the middle of a rainbow!

We began to catch a glimpse of what awaited us – and it boggled our supernatural minds. Having just experienced a thousand years of what we considered near perfection, we had now been introduced to the next level.

---

[98] Revelation 21:16

There would be no concerns in this realm. Never again would we have to contend with even a hint of rebellion to the will of our Creator. The revelation of the infinite majesty and power of God had begun. A universe of exploration awaited us.

And we heard a great voice out of Heaven saying,

"Behold, the tabernacle of God is with men, and He will dwell with them, and they shall be His people, and God Himself shall dwell with them, and be their God."[99]

The Beginning

---

[99] Revelation 21:3

APPENDIX

As I mentioned in the Foreword, this was not meant as a book to teach Biblical theology. There are many applications of Scripture in this book that are from my own imagination and *possible* interpretations of events prophesied to take place during the Millennial Reign of Christ. Having said that, I strove to write in such a way as not to knowingly contradict those things in the Bible that are explicit in their presentation, and indeed the possible interpretations that I have presented have been arrived at through looking at inferences and principles of Scripture. Here is some insight into the thinking that resulted in the presentation of the concepts that you have just read about.

- THE ABILITY OF THE SAINTS TO CHANGE THEIR APPEARANCE, AND TO CHANGE THE WAY THEY AND OTHERS ARE PERCEIVED; THE OTHER SUPERNATURAL ABILITIES OF THE SAINTS

This starts with the idea that who we are is more real than our physical appearance. The essence of who we are does not change as our bodies age. Even if something were to happen to alter our outward appearance, we would still be the same person.

Then we have the passage from I Corinthians 13:12:

"For now we see through a glass, darkly; but then face to face: now I know in part; but then shall I know even as also I am known."

Granted, this does not clearly state what it means that Paul, and by extension we, as believers, will *"know even as (we) are known"*, but it opens the door to the possibility that our knowledge of one another will enter a different realm than the one we experience now, which is compared to looking through a clouded window.

This concept is also bolstered by the abilities that the Lord possessed in His resurrection body. We note that Christ took on various physical forms after His resurrection, appearing to the disciples first in His earthly body, complete with wounds from the nails of the cross and the piercing of His side. He later concealed His identity from the disciples on the road to Emmaus in Luke 24, and then appeared in a much different form to John on the Isle of Patmos, revealing His glory and majesty.

Having seen this ability of the Lord Jesus to alter His physical form after His resurrection, consider these promises made to us concerning <u>our</u> resurrected bodies:

"Beloved, now are we the sons of God, and it doth not yet appear what we shall be: but we know that, when

He shall appear, <u>we shall be like Him; for we shall see Him as He is</u>." – I John 3:2

And one of my favorites:

"For our conversation is in Heaven; from whence also we look for the Savior, the Lord Jesus Christ: who shall change our vile body, that it may be fashioned like unto His glorious body, according to the working whereby He is able even to subdue all things unto Himself." – Philippians 3:20-21

So, if our bodies are going to be like His body, and His body is capable of supernatural acts – including the ability to "subdue all things unto Himself" – I think it is reasonable to assume that we will also be capable of supernatural acts even beyond limits of our imaginations.

Consider finally this passage from I Corinthians 15, as Paul instructs the believers on the resurrection body:

"But some will say, 'How are the dead raised up? And with what body do they come? Thou fool, that which thou sowest is not quickened except it die: and that which thou sowest, thou sowest not that body that shall be, but bare grain, it may chance of wheat, or some other grain: but God giveth it a body as it pleased Him, and to every seed his own body...There are also celestial bodies, and bodies terrestrial: but the glory of

the celestial is one, and the glory of the terrestrial is another...So also is the resurrection of the dead. It is sown in corruption; it is raised in incorruption: it is sown in dishonor; it is raised in glory: it is sown in weakness; it is raised in power: it is sown a natural body; it is raised a spiritual body. There is a natural body, and there is a spiritual body...And as we have born the image of the earthy, we shall also bear the image of the heavenly."

- SOME IN GLORIFIED BODIES, OTHERS NOT IN GLORIFIED BODIES; DIFFERENT CLASSIFICATIONS OF CITIZENS OF THE KINGDOM (SAINTS, ADAMITES, MORTALS)

I should start out by saying that the titles given, particularly "Adamites" and "Mortals" have no Scriptural basis. I chose them to help with the identification of the groups, seeing "Adamites" as linking them to the perfectly created, but not supernatural body, that Adam was originally given, and "Mortals" as indications that these had not yet been given the gift of eternal life, and thus were not immortal.

There are several different theological positions regarding who will receive glorified bodies and who will not. I have taken this position because in Scripture I can only find promises to the Church that they will have glorified bodies. Many may take a different position regarding this, and I would not argue with them.

However, there are definitely some different groups of people who will be dwelling in the Millennial Kingdom. In addition to those saved during the church age, there will also be the Old Testament saints, the tribulation saints, those who will be at the Judgment of the Nations referenced in Matthew 24:31-46, as well as converted Israel.

Some of these will definitely *not* be in glorified bodies, as they will be those who will resist the rule of Christ (addressed in the next section) and be destroyed in the final assault against Him.

The issue of classifications is also linked to the question of children who are born or who mature during the Millennial Kingdom. Assuming that I am correct in the belief that there will indeed be children born and raised during the Kingdom Age (I will address this as I discuss the question of children in the Kingdom), then the questions arise, "Will they be in glorified bodies? And if so, when are they granted them?"

All of these issues lend themselves to speculation that there will be different groups, with possibly different physical manifestations, during the Kingdom Age.

- THERE WILL BE INFANTS AND CHILDREN IN THE KINGDOM; THESE WILL INCLUDE THE SOULS OF THOSE ABORTED OR WHO DIED IN INFANCY

First, as to the presence of infants and children in the Kingdom, there is no doubt. Consider these passages:

"And the sucking child shall play on the hole of the asp, and the weaned child shall put his hand on the cockatrice' den." – Isaiah 11:10

"And the streets of the city shall be full of boys and girls playing in the streets thereof." – Zechariah 8:5

So, we know they will be there. The only question is - where do they come from? Many point to the Scripture in Matthew 22:30 where Jesus said that *"...in the resurrection they neither marry, nor are given in marriage, but are as the angels of God."* From this passage they conclude that there will not be any births, since there will be no marriage.

I choose to believe that this passage applies to the Saints, those in glorified bodies, but not to the other groups that will be there, including the children themselves as they grow up and mature during the thousand years. I therefore believe that the other groups – those not in glorified bodies – will indeed reproduce and be the source of the infants and children identified in these passages.

As to the idea that some of these will be the souls of the aborted millions as well as those who die in infancy, I have no specific Scriptural reference for this. In fact, there is precious little in Scripture that gives definitive information concerning infants who die. Often when confronted with this question we are taken all the way back to David's remarks in II Samuel 12:23 concerning his infant child who had died: *"...Can I bring him back again? I shall go to him, but he shall not return to me."*

I'm sure that part of the reason I take this position is to find some small amount of comfort over the millions whose lives have been sacrificed on the altar of selfishness and sin. I have to believe that a God who is as gracious as our God will somehow make provision for the innocents who never had an opportunity to experience life.

- THERE WILL BE THOSE WHO WILL RESIST THE AUTHORITY OF CHRIST, AND THOSE WHO HAVE NOT ALREADY DONE SO WILL HAVE THE OPPORTUNITY TO ACCEPT OR REJECT THE LORDSHIP OF CHRIST.

Again, as to the first part of this assumption, there is no doubt. There will definitely be those in the Kingdom who will not willfully submit to the authority of Christ. Consider these passages:

"And it shall come to pass, that every one that is left of all the nations which came against Jerusalem shall even go up from year to year to worship the King, the LORD of

hosts, and to keep the feast of tabernacles. And it shall be, that whoso will not come up of all the families of the earth to Jerusalem to worship the King, the LORD of hosts, even upon them shall there be no rain. And if the family of Egypt go not up, and come not, that have no rain; there shall be the plague, wherewith the LORD will smite the heathen that come not up to keep the feast of tabernacles. This shall be the punishment of Egypt, and the punishment of all nations that come not up to keep the feast of tabernacles." – Zechariah 14:16-19*

This certainly refers to a spirit of resistance, even referring to them as "heathen." Then of course, there is the final rebellion:

"And when the thousand years are expired, Satan shall be loosed out of his prison, and shall go out to deceive the nations which are in the four quarters of the earth, Gog and Magog, to gather them together to battle: the number of whom is as the sand of the sea." – Revelation 20:8

So, there will definitely be those during the Kingdom Age who will resist and ultimately rebel against the authority of Christ. How about the assumption that they will have an opportunity to accept the rule of Christ, and that this will be necessary for them to be given the gift of eternal life and live beyond the end of the Millennial Reign?

These assumptions flow naturally for me from two principles that I see presented in Scripture.

1) God desires the death of no man, desiring that all will repent and turn to Him.

"The Lord is not slack concerning His promise, as some men count slackness; but is longsuffering to us-ward, not willing that any should perish, but that all should come to repentance." – II Peter 3:9

"...As I live, saith the Lord God, I have no pleasure in the death of the wicked; but that the wicked turn from his way and live: turn ye, turn ye from your evil ways; for why will ye die, O house of Israel?" – Ezekiel 33:11

2) No one will be saved apart from faith in Jesus Christ and submission to Him.

"For God so loved the world, that He gave His only begotten Son, that whosoever <u>believeth on Him</u> should not perish, but have everlasting life...He that believeth on Him is not condemned: but he that believeth not is condemned already, because he hath not believed in the name of the only begotten Son of God." – John 3:16, 18

"<u>Except a man be born again</u>, he cannot see the kingdom of God."
– John 3:3

"He that believeth on the Son hath everlasting life: and he that believeth not the Son shall not see life; but the wrath of God abideth on Him." – John 3:36

"...if thou shalt confess with thy mouth the Lord Jesus, and shalt believe in thine heart that God hath raised Him from the dead, thou shalt be saved. For with the heart man believeth unto righteousness; and with the mouth confession is made unto salvation." – Romans 10:9-10

From these two principles comes the idea that those alive during the Kingdom age must choose, just as we have chosen, to surrender ourselves fully to Christ.

- **THE AGING PROCESS SLOWED DOWN DURING THE KINGDOM AGE**

This is one of my two favorite "imaginations". I have no specific Scripture references that state this, but the idea came from one observation and one Scripture passage.

The observation has to do with the creation as it was originally, up until the time of the great flood of Noah's day. We are all aware that people lived much longer lives – several hundred years, even approaching one thousand years old. But I also noticed something else about the records of their lives.

If you study the genealogy recorded in Genesis 5, not only do you see records of extremely long lives, but you will notice that the age of child bearing is also extremely old. The youngest age given for what we presume to be the birth of a man's first son is sixty-five years old! (Mahalaleel, verse 15, and Enoch, verse 21) Methuselah, on the other hand, was 187 years old when he sired Lamech! (Verse 25)

This certainly seems to indicate to me that not only did people live longer, but that the maturing and aging processes were considerably slower. Since we will live for a thousand years in the Kingdom on a perfected earth, it seemed reasonable to me that the aging process might revert back to the way it was when the creation was also perfect.

Then there is this Scripture reference:
"There shall be no more thence an infant of days, nor an old man that hath not filled his days: for the child shall die an hundred years old: but the sinner being an hundred years old shall be accursed." – Isaiah 65:20

While I'm not sure about all that verse entails, it does speak of a 100-year-old child!

- **REVERTING TO OUR PHYSICAL BODIES DURING THE OBSERVANCE OF FEAST OF TABERNACLES**

This is the second of my two favorite "imaginations". Again, I have no specific Scripture references that lead me to this conclusion.

The idea originally occurred to me while studying the Feast of Tabernacles, and the significance of how and why the Jews were instructed to observe it. It was to be for them a time of remembrance – a time when they would live in the types of dwellings that they inhabited when they were wandering in the wilderness because of their unbelief.

We are specifically told that the Feast of Tabernacles will be observed forever, and specifically during the Kingdom age. (Leviticus 23:41; Zechariah 14:16) As I thought about our observance of the Feast of Tabernacles, I asked myself, "How will we as Gentiles observe it? Living in a tent for seven days would have no significance to us since we did not have the history that Israel had of living in tents during their sojourn in the wilderness."

So, how does that relate to our sojourn? Then I look at what Paul had to say in II Corinthians 5:

"For we know that if our earthly house of this tabernacle were dissolved, we have a building of God, an house not made with hands, eternal in the heavens. For in this we groan, earnestly desiring to be clothed with our house which is from Heaven: if so be that being clothed we shall not be found naked. For we that are in this tabernacle do groan, being burdened: not that we would be unclothed, but clothed upon, that mortality might be swallowed up of life."

I find it intriguing that the word translated "tabernacle" is actually the word "tent". We are actually dwelling in a "tent", a temporary dwelling during our entire sojourn in this life. Further, the reason we are in such a flimsy house while we are here on earth is a result of sin and disobedience, just as Israel's sojourn in the wilderness.

If Israel was to dwell in tents for seven days to remind them of what happens when we disobey God, and what God delivered them from, then it makes sense to me that we might have to spend some time in our "tents" while observing the Feast of Tabernacles.

- BANISHMENTS

Again, no specific Scripture reference. We are told that Christ and His representatives will rule with "a rod of iron".

"And he that overcometh, and keepeth My works unto the end, to him will I give power over the nations: and he shall rule them with a rod of iron; as the vessels of a potter shall they be broken to shivers: even as I received of My Father." – Revelation 2:26-27

This certainly indicates that there will be severe judgments meted out for the rebellious during the ruling of Christ's followers over the nations. As to what form this might take, there are few details in Scripture.

So, there you have it. I'll say one more time - this was not intended as a theological exercise. I do not maintain that every depiction contained in this book will be carried out exactly as described – far from it. But hopefully it has given you some new perspective with which to look at Scripture and allow your mind to open up to the unlimited possibilities that exist in the mind of an infinite and omnipotent Creator. I truly believe the wonders that we will behold and the adventures that await us far exceed anything that I have portrayed.

See you in the Kingdom!